- Nobody is perfect.
- All I can do is my best.
- Making a mistake does not mean I am stupid or a failure. It only means that I am human. Everyone makes mistakes!
- Its OK not to be pleasant all the time. Everyone has a bad day sometimes.
- Its OK if some people don't like me. No one is liked by everyone.

Learn to view situations as other people might see them.

"What might I tell a close friend who was having similar thoughts?"

ASK:

1. does it really matter?
2. what's the worst that could happen?
3. Will this matter tomorrow? next week? next year?

"What level of imperfection am I willing to tolerate?"

ALSO BY KATE BOWLER

The Lives We Actually Have: 100 Blessings for Imperfect Days (with Jessica Richie)

Good Enough: 40ish Devotionals for a Life of Imperfection (with Jessica Richie)

No Cure for Being Human: And Other Truths I Need to Hear

The Preacher's Wife: The Precarious Power of Evangelical Women Celebrities

Everything Happens for a Reason: And Other Lies I've Loved

Blessed: A History of the American Prosperity Gospel

Have a Beautiful, Terrible Day!

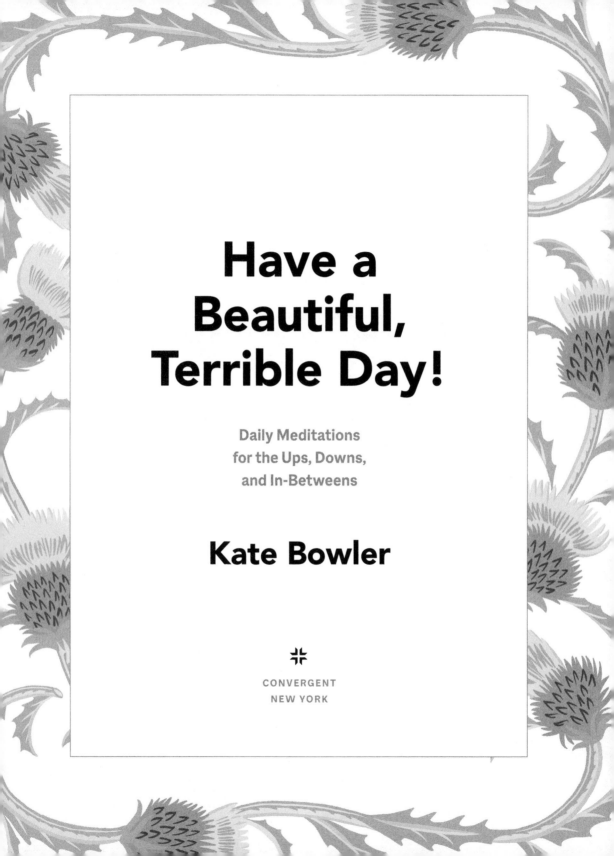

Have a Beautiful, Terrible Day!

Daily Meditations
for the Ups, Downs,
and In-Betweens

Kate Bowler

CONVERGENT
NEW YORK

Published in the United States by Convergent Books, an imprint of
Random House, a division of Penguin Random House LLC, New York.

CONVERGENT BOOKS is a registered trademark and the Convergent
colophon is a trademark of Penguin Random House LLC.

Scripture credits are located on page 203.

Hardback ISBN 9780593727676
Ebook ISBN 9780593727683

PRINTED IN THE UNITED STATES OF AMERICA
ON ACID-FREE PAPER

convergentbooks.com

1st Printing

First Edition

dedication

There have been long stretches when I could not carry the weight of my life. And it caused me no end of embarrassment. But do you know the cure for that kind of shame?

Roger.

Roger Loyd was the librarian at Duke Divinity School, a United Methodist pastor, husband and father, and the guy who drove me to the airport at 3:30 A.M. on Wednesdays to get cancer treatment in another state. I would kiss my sleeping baby on the forehead and get in his car, and he would have to tell me to stop talking at least three times because I was already exhausting myself trying to be charming (but was I *actually* charming? Unclear). It was a stupid time of night/early morning, and I felt guilty that he was always volunteering for dumb errands that would prevent me from trying to live with the independence I preferred.

Roger was not nearly old enough when he died, and now there is a bolt missing in the machinery that holds the universe together. He is certainly in heaven being incredibly useful and he would hate the spotlight of this dedication. But let me just say, Roger, before you ask me to stop talking, *Thank you.*

And thank you to all the Rogers who keep the universe humming. This book is for you.

contents

Have a Beautiful, Terrible Lent!

Have a Beautiful, Terrible Advent!

preface

These are terrible days. These are beautiful days. Somehow both realities feel inseparable in our minds now.

We have the sense that something bad might happen, and has already happened. When we read the headlines, we do not shake our heads. We nod. *Yes,* we think. *Of course that would happen.*

Our moods seem tight and jittery. We worry about groceries and school shootings and airborne viruses. We worry about kids and parents and friends and whether this, whatever *this* is, is all we can expect. We worry about the heart-stopping events we have already endured and what will happen next.

We worry about how we will get it all done.

We worry about everything that can never be undone.

"How are you?" people ask us.

"Anxious," we might reply.

But when the sun begins its nightly descent, instinctively, we cast our eyes to the horizon. We have the sense that something lovely will happen, and has already happened yesterday. We notice how the white glare of the sun behind starched clouds is pooling into oranges and deep reds, and our breath begins to slow. We nod. *Yes, we think. This is also what happens.*

Our moods thaw into awe. We marvel at good medicine, the invention of cheese dip, and the delightful mischief in our child's eye no matter how old they are. We marvel at the intricacy of flowers and the ingenuity of cities built from steel and concrete. We cannot believe how much our parents can drive us bananas and our friends can make us laugh so hard that we need to find a wall to support ourselves.

We find ourselves surrounded by the daily miracles of planets turning and stars blinking and people who hug us when we come through the door.

"How are you?" people ask us.

"Grateful," we might reply.

We might feel awful or wonderful, but we are running out of those middle-of-the-road feelings . . . the more boring, humdrum feelings of being unfazed by the world around us. We are no longer able to be carried along by the momentum of ordinary days unfolding into other ordinary days. Instead, we are lifted and carried by currents larger than we are, taking us further and faster than we wanted to go. There are highs and lows, soaring views and stomach-clenching drops.

This is the new way of being in the world, the sense of unpredictably and precipitously rising and falling. We are made of feathers. We are made of stone.

What Kind of Anxiety Is This?

Why do we feel fear pricking at the edges of our minds? Why does it feel so normal to be so hypervigilant . . . so *aware*?

Well, there are a few varieties of fear that might be useful to name here: apocalyptic awareness, anxious awareness, and awareness of pain. And none of these emotions will be the sort of thing we bring up at parties, but we intuitively understand them to be parts of how we experience worry.

Apocalyptic Awareness

The first, apocalyptic awareness, will not be news to you. We feel afraid because—to name only a few factors—we are witnessing the increasing fragility of the structures that hold up our lives. We are seeing all the signs of our weakening democracy, the eroding environment, racial injustice, public mistrust of civic institutions, the rise of medical bankruptcy, et cetera . . . I could go on and on. We feel afraid because the headlines break into our days like sledgehammers.

When we start to feel like our world is teetering on the edge of the abyss, we are living with a sense of the apocalypse. *Apocalyptic* is a wonderful word because it feels the way it sounds: destructive, terrifying, catastrophic. But the word also means "that which is revealed."

(Side note: Theologically speaking, Christians have a long, rich tradition of thinking and arguing and making predictions about the way God's creation—the earth and everything else made by divine intent—comes to an end. E.g., Jesus returning to earth, AND SO ON. But I don't mean *apocalyptic* in that narrow sense.)

It's also the feeling we get when we watch a documentary about rising sea levels and experience a chill. We feel like we are staring over the edge of time itself. Something happens in our minds. We pick up the thought and then want to drop it immediately because it is too impossible, too big, and too terrible to imagine. We worry that nothing we do would matter anyway. *And yet we know. We see.* We can't pull our eyes away.

Anxious Awareness

Some of us—most of us—would probably say that we know less about downright terror and more about anxiety. We wear it like a second skin. What could happen? Will it happen? We find ourselves guessing and second-guessing choices we have made. We lose more time stopping and checking our impulses than we could possibly describe, only because we would have to stop and check to think about it first. Other people seem to have a kind of natural bravado that propels them through life (which, sorry for my loud judgments here, makes them brave or stupid or wildly efficient). But that's not us.

Our thoughts have an endlessness to them: *What does that person think? What should I do? What did I do wrong? How can I keep myself safe? How can I keep others safe?* We don't know how to protect ourselves from the feeling that we are exposed somehow, open to the elements. We understand vigilance intimately. We would be naked without it.

Painful Awareness

For some of us, our relationship with fear is locked inside our own bodies and daily experiences. Many of us feel afraid because we are swimming through physical and emotional pain—the kind of pain that threatens to wash us all away. We are immersed in the feeling of the ongoing and never-ending tragedy of our circumstances. Other people seem to belong to another world—a world where people think about dinner and chitchat about whether there will be rain or snow later on in the week. It turns out that there will always be rain or snow later on in the week, so they will keep talking. Meanwhile, we barely have language at all.

We lose the ability to arrange and rearrange thoughts that could make sense of what is happening to us and why. We would run, but where would we go? It's happening inside of us or to us.

We try crying, we try talking, we try silence. We try sleeping, we try screaming, we try telling a friend. We eat ourselves sick. We starve ourselves empty. Nothing works entirely. Everything works a little. The claustrophobia of this tragedy is suffocating. But then during the stray moments, we forget. The normalcy we glimpse feels like a delusion. *What is more real than this pain? What is truer about me than this?*

Living in the Beautiful, Terrible

Something you should know about me: I wrote this particular book now because I am in the midst of a dark season of pain. I have physical pain that ripples down my back and pelvis, up and down my legs, and crawls up my neck. It feels cold and loud. It feels like lightning delivered intravenously, washing over me in waves.

I almost never talk about it, because I find pain difficult to describe and even more difficult to describe over and over again to people who love me and cannot help me. (I am not recommending this kind of inwardness, only confessing that I haven't figured out another way.) So, rightly or wrongly, I don't talk about pain, but I think about it on a thirty-second loop. Driving, scrubbing dishes, doing laundry, talking to friends, taking meetings, answering email, talking on the phone. Some days the pain is so deafening that I forget what room I'm in. People are talking and I can't quite make out the words. I worry that the look on my face will give away how far I have drifted from where they can reach me. I am lost to myself, given over to a body that is deeply indifferent about what I put on the calendar.

But I discovered that for roughly an hour first thing in the morning, my brain was bright and clear. So I wrote these blessings and reflections. It was all I could do. I couldn't research long-term history books (as I am often doing). I couldn't write long-form stories because that, friends, takes hours and hours and I had only a short burst before my ability to think detonated. But I could say:

God, whatever is true about you had better be true now.

Today.

I could not wait until tomorrow to have long, luxurious thoughts about the Christian past and some hypothetically wonderful person I might become if I could only get my act together. Instead, if I wanted to pray or bless this day, I needed to be able to place my faith alongside my reality. And my reality is fear, pain, and fear *of* pain.

If you are anxious or worried about whether your life can also be beautiful, welcome. Me too. Thank you for joining me here. I can't tell you how nice it is to have company when, otherwise, I would assume the social media lie that everyone is living a spectacular and effortless life drinking green smoothies somewhere, doing beachfront yoga or noodling around Europe, is true.

What I want more than anything is to bless you and me right now, and feel the truth of our realities without letting reality itself overwhelm us. People often say, "FAITH NOT FEAR," as if faithful people can't be afraid. But we are afraid for so many reasons, many of them both reasonable and realistic. So let's just settle that controversy now: we can be faithful and afraid at the same time.

Awareness Is Your Gift

Let's try talking about faith and fear in the same breath. Oooohhh, this feels a little spicy but I'm going to argue it anyway. I want to suggest that being a Christian *encourages us* to understand fear in a more intimate way.

Let me tell you a story about roofs. And about why we know something good about faith and fear and love and Christianity, maybe because of them.

I was twenty-five. It was in the cowboy days of subprime mortgage lending, and a bank was dumb enough to give me, a graduate student in religion, enough money to purchase a bungalow in Durham, North Carolina. My husband and I had recently moved to the United States from Canada, so our credit scores were purely hypothetical, and the hilariously small stipend that I received for teaching, researching, and correctly pronouncing Kierkegaard's name to my classmates (no, look, it's really more like Kierke*gore*) furnished us with a lot of stories in the years to come about the time we got vitamin deficiencies and all the skin on my husband's hands inexplicably peeled off. But we had a house we couldn't afford, which was still a treat, and the previous owner had left a bright green mini-golf carpet in the living room, and an entire Elvis Presley tribute room in what later became our guest room.

There was a shed in the backyard with all kinds of promise—a simple peaked structure, two floors high, and lined with thick white oak. It had been a carpenter's workshop for the owner who had built the main house and who had even bothered to line the edges of the property with elegant masonry quarried from the same bluish gray stone that made my school, Duke University, look like Duke University. But the problem with the shed was the crater where the roof had sunk so low that termites and wet wood were threatening to pull the whole thing down. We tried to prop it up as best we could—beams here, brackets there—but the only real solution would be a religious one.

I have always believed that one of the great arguments for being part of a collectivist Christian tradition—three cheers for Mennonites, Hutterites, Amish, and Anabaptists of all kinds—is their willingness to do voluntary, grueling manual labor and call it love. And we would need a lot of love. So our Mennonite family drove the thirty-seven hours from their prairie homes in Canada and took residence in the King of Rock and Roll's Memorial Room (as we had begun to call the guest room). They used reciprocating saws for most of the day until their biceps burned and not much of the original building was left. Then they measured new wood and we bought a nail gun, and sometimes, at night, I would wake up to find my husband flicking me in the head in his sleep because his hand, the nail gun, had a lot of work left to do.

That year the star of the Christmas letter was the shed, with a few addenda to make clear that it should last another twenty-five years before it caved in again on account of the limited warranty on the shingles. I thought about this often when I would sit in the yard, watching the same people show up to build me a fence because I had recently received a sudden Stage IV cancer diagnosis and there was nothing else to do. I wondered about the shed, which would almost certainly outlive me now, and how all my plans (oh, my lovely plans) had been stripped down to the studs.

If you asked me before the cancer, before the years of treatment and stacks of medical bills, I would have told you almost nothing about fear or anxiety or the headlines of the newspaper. I would have told you, one way or another, that I don't need to be terribly afraid because *I am a sure thing. I'm a great bet. Look at me, quieting fear with my tidy individualism and my store-bought solutions.* Fear is for people, other people, who can't ensure their own future.

Human lives really do seem like very sensible projects when you initially add them up. A golden anniversary is fifty years and possibly two kids and three furnaces. A retirement home for your parents is at least another monthly mortgage payment for a decade, but you can probably budget correctly if you imagine finally paying off your student loans. And then taking out another. We add and subtract for radiators and replacement cars and when the dishwasher vomits all the soapy, dirty water onto the hardwood floor (but only when we are on vacation). We don't feel lucky, but we are.

What I had not learned from my shed caving in in the first place was what Simone de Beauvoir calls our "facticity." All of our freedoms—our choices and our ridiculous attempts to plan our lives—are constrained by so many unchangeable details. I was born in this particular year to those parents in this town. This medication exists and that treatment doesn't, but now it seems that all along I had these cancer cells in my colon, spreading to my liver, and scattered in my abdomen because of a genetic blueprint written long ago.

This existential state is, to borrow a term from Martin Heidegger, the *thrownness* of human life. As we wake to the suffering of this world and our own existence, we find ourselves hurtling through time. We reach out for something, anything, to steady us, but we are like astronauts untethered. That is a particular kind of grief—the awareness that we are not drivers of our circumstances, not anymore. We are unwilling passengers.

Willing to Be Carried

American culture values choice above all. People who choose are masters of their own destiny. They are the greatest of all mythical creatures: self-made. By contrast, people with fewer choices—less independence, more dependence—might begin to feel the sting of a distinct kind of shame. We might wonder if our awareness of our limitations is a sign of our failures. After all, we have failed to render ourselves invincible and carry our own weight. We stumbled and did not always recover; we took and could not always give.

Even at my most durable, I should have seen that it took so many people to build my life, prop it up, and maintain it. But once I was sick, I came to realize that a failure to live life on my own is not a failure at all.

The hard truth is that the most basic aspect of our humanity is not our determination, our talents, or whatever we accomplished during last year's resolutions. We are united by our fragility. We all need shelter because we are soft and mushy and irritable in the elements— and we will need so much more than a bank loan because, sooner or later, we are left exposed. Time and chance, says the author of Ecclesiastes, happen to us all.

Honestly, none of us can afford the lives we already have. We set out to build our own dreams, slay our own dragons, and pay our own taxes, and find that we trip over our health and our marriages and the way our inboxes suck us into the void. We were promised that American individualism and a multibillion-dollar self-help industry would set us on our feet. When North Americans look for answers to our dependence, we often turn to the easy promises of the gospel of self-help: "Try harder!" "Change your mindset." "You are your greatest hope." So we bought cheap paperbacks in a frenzy to find a cure for being human.

But soon our own limitations—and the weakness of our institutions—showed us the absurdity of this kind of individualism. (It was the atomism that French sociologist Alexis de Tocqueville, that early astute observer of American culture, warned us about.) Our dreams turned out to be built from toothpicks, each person propped up to stand entirely alone.

We understand instinctively that we cannot win this game of solitaire. Our churches and book clubs, bible studies, farmers' markets, and our carpools and sports teams offer little reminders that we should need each other, borrow and lend money, babysit and run an errand, argue and debate.

"Absolute independence is a false ideal," argued the sociologist Robert Bellah, whose deep understanding of the invention of the modern self rarely missed the mark. "It delivers not the autonomy it promises but loneliness and vulnerability instead."

But we usually see this only when we have sunk to the very bottom. Pastor Nadia Bolz-Weber described how she understood the truth of interdependence most fully when she began practicing the uncomfortable honesty demanded by Alcoholics Anonymous.

"Recovery is hard to do on your own," she observed. "You have to do it with a group of other people who are messed up in the same way but have found some light in their darkness. Sitting in those rooms in twelve-step meetings, there's a particular kind of hope that only comes from being in the midst of people who have really suffered—suffered at their own hand—who can be completely and totally honest about that."

Her group nicknamed this sort of community "The Rowing Club." They would have to take turns pulling on the oar. At times, each would have to be willing to be carried.

A Delightfully Christian Word: Precarity

There is an absolutely spot-on word to describe this way of being in the world, its fragility, its dependence. And I would be delighted if you began to use it in your daily life and especially at work events. That word is *precarity*.

The English word *precarity* means a state of dangerous uncertainty, but its Latin root tells us a good deal more about its Christian character. The term comes from *precarious* or "obtained by entreaty or prayer"—a state where we cannot achieve things by ourselves. We must rely on someone else, God or neighbor.

So instead of saying that we are self-mastering winners, beautiful cyborgs who can somehow rule our worlds by our own determination, we can admit truths that are much more realistic. How are we? Dependent. How are we doing? Fine until we need help (which will be in roughly two or three minutes).

This understanding offers us a more comfortable relationship between our faith and our fear. Our fear is an awareness of the world and our place in it. And what are we? Fragile.

There is a wonderful, saintly Catholic woman you should get to know if you haven't already; her name is Dorothy Day. She lived in New York City in the slums with people who couldn't afford adequate food and shelter. One day she received a letter from a priest from the Caribbean island of Martinique describing his own work with the poor, and the letter was quite pointed about what it would mean for all those of us wanting stable roofs.

He wrote: "Here we want precarity in everything except the church." In other words, we talk a good game about wanting to be people who love what God loves until it requires that we begin to accept anxiety and fear as part of the life of faith. The priest went on to say that recently the place where they were handing out food was nearly collapsing and they had tried to prop it up with several supplemental poles. But it would last maybe only two or three more years. "Someday it will fall on our heads and that will be funny," he said drily. But he couldn't bring himself to stop feeding people in the breadlines in order to be another kind of church, the kind that was "always building, enlarging, and embellishing." We have no right to, he concluded. No right, I suppose he meant, to demand security afforded to no one else.

As Christians we must nod our heads and shrug our shoulders when we're told, in no uncertain terms, that there are no lifetime warranties.

Our Delicate Selves

There is a tremendous opportunity here, now, for us to develop language and foster community around empathy, courage, and hope in the midst of this fear of our own vulnerability. Our neighbors are expressing an aching desire to feel less alone, needing language for the pain they've experienced, searching for meaning and someone to tell them the truth. They are hungry for honesty in the age of shellacked social media influencers. They are desperate for a thicker kind of hope that can withstand their circumstances and embolden them to preach the truth of our resurrected Lord, whose future kingdom will have no tears and no pain and no Instagram at all.

We have a few good clues that we are allowed to hope for this kind of interreliance here, now. There's a strange story in the gospel of Luke about friends who bring one of their own to see Jesus. Their Rowing Club was a man down, so they carried him to where Jesus was preaching in the hope that he could be healed from his paralysis. But the crowds were thick and the friends couldn't get through the door, so they had a dangerous idea and climbed onto the roof and began to dismantle it. Then they lowered their friend through the tiles on a stretcher into the middle of the bewildered throng. And then, and then, and then, a miracle happened. (And if you haven't read the story, it's in Luke 5 and the surprise ending is lovely. The paralyzed man gets up and walks. Go read it and pretend I didn't spoil it already.)

It is a miracle when we let ourselves, in desperation, be lowered into the unknown. When we let ourselves cry or scream or even whisper that we fear our own undoing. We will have almost nothing in our control except the knowledge of our fragility, and we will watch someone else wear themselves out running to the pharmacist or cleaning the bathrooms and sanding a plank of wood for yet another Anabaptist form of love.

It is a miracle when we see the precarity of others and we decide to carry the weight of their stretchers instead of worrying about the groceries. God bless all the people who bothered with my complaints and worried about my heartbreak. The saints are those who press pause on louder concerns because they have decided to remember what they would rather forget: our independence is a sham.

And it would be the greatest miracle of all to be the paralyzed man who gets off the stretcher. Who hears Jesus's voice returning us to ourselves. We are healed. We are whole. We came through the roof but we walked out the door. Hallelujah.

If I am very lucky, the shingles will last and the chemotherapy will hold and the pain will quiet and love will continue to do most of the work. I will go back to being someone who tallies up the inconvenient expiry dates of large appliances and count birthdays and new years to set the clock of my mortality. I will be like the homeowner an hour after Jesus and the crowd have left, my floor littered with broken tiles and crumbled plaster.

And I will look up, through the gaping hole, to the blue, blue sky right from where I stand, no longer surprised by the fundamental Christian truth that the roof always, always caves in.

How to Use This Book

This book contains small reflections and blessings that, I hope, will set the dial correctly on our daily fears and anxieties.

We want to be aware and not overwhelmed.

We want to allow love to be more real than our catastrophizing.

We want to be awake to the world but chill enough to be good to a friend when they have problems with their combination washer-dryer. (After all, we can't always be yelling about precarity.)

These daily entries are meant to be thumbed through, picked up and set down when you need them. Please do not ever, ever, ever feel bad that you did not read them beginning to end. I have never successfully done a devotional book in chronological order, so let me free you of that guilt. But if you are the kind of person who likes a little discipline, go at your chosen pace. Take what you need. The chapters have been descriptively labeled in the table of contents so that you can find the themes that might match what you are going through.

I have made a plan for those of you who might want to use this book during Advent (the time leading up to Christmas), Christmastide, and Lent (the time leading up to Jesus's death and resurrection). Those are the Big Stories in the Christian calendar, and sometimes it's nice to have a routine to include them in your spiritual life.

Have a Beautiful, Terrible Day!

A few years ago, around Lent, I realized I didn't have the right way to say, "Bless us in this new way of being." So I started saying, "Have a beautiful, terrible day!" It made me laugh and it felt, well, honest.

So here's to us having beautiful, terrible days. And here's a little blessing as we do:

Blessed are we, the anxious,

with eyes wide open to the lovely and the awful.

Blessed are we, the aware,

knowing that the only sane thing to do in such a world

is to admit the fear that sits in our peripheral vision.

Blessed are we, the hopeful,

eyes searching for the horizon,

ready to meet the next miracle, the next surprise.

Yes, blessed are we, the grateful,

awake to this beautiful, terrible day.

Have a Beautiful, Terrible Day!

Here is the world.

Beautiful and terrible things will happen.

Don't be afraid.

—FREDERICK BUECHNER

when everything is out of control

Give me a sign of your goodness.

—PSALM 86:17A (NIV)

There is something people say when you are in a lot of pain or trouble or life is out of control. They say: "All you can control is your reaction." And, sure, that's often good advice. We can try to reduce the scale of our problem-solving to a small, manageable step. But I don't want you to have to skip that first true thing you are allowed to say: "I have lost control. This is happening *to* me." This blessing is for when you need to say, "God, this is out of control. People keep telling me that I have control over this, but I really don't. I need help." Read or pray this meditation aloud if you need some divine rescue plan and some acknowledgment of that reality.

All you can change, they say, is you.
You don't control anyone but yourself.
All you can do, they say,
is take a breath and
consider your reaction
to what is happening.
Return to yourself.
You are what is happening.

What is happening is a landslide, God.
The world melted before my eyes.
It is the feeling of my feet going first
then my back, smack against the ground
then the *whooshing* sound
of the earth as it moves.

It's the speed.
God, why didn't anyone tell me
about the speed at which it goes—
my horizon, my choices, my control—
before, *blink, blink,*
someone with a calm voice
is asking me about my reaction
to a world now left behind.

You are there, somewhere out there,
though I can hardly feel it.
Send an angel, send a fleet, send them now.

reflection prompt
A long time ago I started believing (mistakenly)
that I wasn't allowed to ask for help. Is there
someone you can reach out to and tell them
what you're going through?

you're not sleeping much

I will both lie down in peace, and sleep; For You alone, O Lord, make me dwell in safety.

—PSALM 4:8 (NKJV)

When I was young I could never sleep peacefully. I would hover in that place between dreaming and awareness, caught in the webs of restless dreams. Some were absurd (where is the last piece of that puzzle?). Others were terrifying (I can't get out! I can never get out!). I would pace the house—mostly still asleep—in my red pajamas, worrying, worrying, worrying. As an adult, I still have never really gotten the hang of sleep. I lie there thinking, rehearsing, planning, despairing.

This verse from the psalmist has become a precious one to me. It says to me: *Lord, you care even about this waking and sleeping self, the one who no one knows but you.*

Nearby someone is snoring
with the efficiency of
an industrial meat grinder
and it's not polite to hate someone
while their eyes are closed.

Or sometimes the bed is empty,
they are gone, gone,
missing and missed
and there's no use being grateful,
for their silence now takes up
all the oxygen anyhow.

God, no one knows me like this.
Moving from my concrete days,
my immovable schedule,
to nights when I unravel in long loops
like a knitted sweater.

I am someone else entirely.
Needy and hazy, lonely and yet
desperate to be alone.

God, I need the sort of peace
that calms storms into bathtub water.
Or the peace that folds origami
out of the tight corners of my mind.

I need peace like a weighted blanket,
a hand over my heart,
and this time you say it.
You say it like an oath.
You promise.
You will not leave me here, like this,
at the edge of where
darkness meets darkness
while the rest sleep soundly on.

---

reflection prompt
*Find a notepad or blank note on your phone.
List three worries. Don't judge them. No one
has to see them. Now put them away and see if
your mind can drift a little further than before.*

when you're trapped in the past

If I go up to the heavens, you are there; if I make my bed in the depths, you are there.

—PSALM 139:8 (NIV)

The strangest aspect of a tragedy is how it can feel like it happened yesterday, even if it was years ago. (Proving, once again, that we can rarely say "Time heals all wounds!" with any confidence.) And many of us have had hard experiences that begin to feel like layers of sediment, one on top of the other. We can start to feel weighed down. Trapped. Buried alive. It reminds me of how C. S. Lewis described hell as a locked room, a room perhaps locked from the inside.

If you are starting to worry that the hurts of the past are making you feel claustrophobic, let's try to get a little light in that room. This blessing imagines that revisiting our pain can feel like living in an old museum filled with what has happened. Let's picture it and try to imagine that God is there. God is there when we are hurt. God is there when hurts are new or even when they are so old they bore people because we keep bringing them up. (*Well, I wouldn't be bringing it up if it didn't still hurt, people!*) So let's consider our own "museums" for a moment and see if we can open some windows.

The flurry of dust particles
once invisible midair
have formed a thin film
over an inalterable fact:
my wounds are old now.

I used to find a terrible comfort
in fresh rage and tears—
this *just* happened
—but time burned this urgency
to a dull ash.

When you find me you'll notice that
I've opened a museum.
Pay the admission at the door
(it's a token, any kindness really)
and I'll tell you all about
this person here, and that person there,
and who laughed and who didn't.
And what great losses moved everything
out of the house and into boxes only to be
displayed here for your general interest.

But every feeling is cold to the touch.

Bless me, God, crowded out
by all that I've endured.
Unburden me, packed so tightly
in the memories of those
who loved me best
(and worst, if I'm being honest).
Relieve me of every fresh wave of guilt
of all I've already forgotten.

Bless me with enough forgetfulness
to notice the way the sun
is demanding another day
and you can mind the storehouse
of all I've loved
while there's time to gather more.

---

reflection prompt

*Some of our old hurts become stories we retell
without thinking. Is there a story you're
retelling that isn't getting enough genuine
attention? Try to bring it up again with
someone you really trust to listen. You might
say: "I know you've heard this before, but I'm
still really hurting."*

not your best self

**Search me, O God,
and know my heart:
try me, and know my
thoughts.**

—PSALM 139:23 (KJV)

I know we prefer to be lovely, kind, and tra-la-la-la, but sometimes we are not exactly who we hoped. I like to pretend, for example, that I have never given someone the middle finger in traffic. (Reader: I have.) I have said and done things that weren't only wrong, but I love to justify them. Let me quickly tell you all about when that person cut me off in traffic and I was scared and mad and . . .

We are not the people we hoped to be. And our faults are not simply cute stories but deep fault lines that run through every attempt to be transformed into someone changed by God and each other. So, here's a blessing of acknowledgment. We are not who we hoped we would be, but there is so much grace for that.

God, I can't tell
which person
I will be today:
kind and loving,
turn-the-other-cheek and I'll-be-right-here,
soft but strong.
I will keep no record of wrongs.

I might be someone else entirely:
brittle and judgmental,
I'm-taking-my-share and
you-deal-with-it-alone,
hard but weak.
I will keep every record, *dammit*.

I am an accountant in this world
that does not give me what I'm owed.

God, these multiple selves, you know
(of course you know) are parts of a whole.

You send the love I have to give.
You grieve the pain that
causes me to withhold.
You send your spirit every day
not to stitch us back together
but to heal every tender part
from the inside out.

So, in the meantime,
bless this generous self,
bless this breakable self,
bless these many parts and
make them whole.

reflection prompt

If this prayer fails to inspire you, just take the advice I get from Jessica Richie, my frequent coauthor and one of my best friends. "Look, sometimes you just need to eat a banana and take a walk."

when it's not fair
(it really isn't)

The Lord is near to the brokenhearted.

—PSALM 34:18A (NRSVUE)

In the midst of the worst things that have happened to me, I realized that no one was going to show up to apologize. People who have hurt us rarely apologize. Natural disasters and disease will most certainly never say sorry. And even though it felt silly to say "I want an apology" about my cancer diagnosis, I really did. So if you need one too, here's a blessing for when life isn't fair. And, for what it's worth, I'm really sorry that happened to you.

The last time anyone let me say it—
tears in my eyes, straight from the heart—
I was a child.

Didn't anyone tell you?
Life isn't fair.

So I swallow it up.

But, God, without hearing you say it—
"My love, this isn't fair"—
I am heartsick.

I ate this sadness and
it became embarrassment;
I ate this disappointment
and it became bitterness.

God, let me hear you again say,
"My love, this isn't fair."

You will give me strength
to take another step
and courage to face my circumstances.
But, before the doing and trying
and getting-back-up,
you simply look at me and say,
"I love you. I'm sorry.
Let me bless this heartsick day."

---

reflection prompt

*Many of us were raised with a "suck it up"
philosophy. Being deeply tough has probably
been a good gift to you, so thank yourself for
doing that hard work. But then, perhaps, you
might add: "I'm really sorry it's been so hard."
Sometimes compassion is the gift we give
ourselves.*

not drowning in other people's problems

Try to have a sane estimate of your capabilities by the light of the faith that God has given to you all. For just as you have many members in one physical body and those members differ in their functions, so we, though many in number, compose one body in Christ.

—ROMANS 12:4 (PHILLIPS)

Chances are that you take care of someone else too. Your life is not simply yours to shape, but your days and weeks and years are tangled up in the days and weeks and years of another person's needs. This is where a story of American self-determinism really breaks down. We don't shape our own destinies very often. We are incredibly busy worrying about those we love who are very old or very young or who have unfixable problems.

But sometimes we can get so overwhelmed by the needs of others that we feel like we disappear. And it might feel selfish to think about our own needs. Consider this lovely thought by the monk Thomas Merton, whose insights into the spiritual life have been a beacon to so many. He wrote: "Our vocation is not simply to be, but to work together with God in the creation of our own life, our own identity, our own destiny." In other words, we are called not only into creating a life for others, but also into creating our own life and identity.

God, I am a shape-shifter.
Hidden in plain sight.
A great disappearing act.

Every now and again,
when I am spinning in a tornado
of other people's needs and wants,
I worry that if I stepped out of it
to stand dumbfounded for a moment,
my body would cast no shadow.

God, I vanish.
The unnecessary pain
and necessary needs
of others feel durable. Measurable.
God, look at how much they need me.
Isn't it necessary that I am
not myself today?

God, remind me of my own goodness.
The way you look at me and grin.
The way the earth can stretch to hold
my own dreams when I remember them.

God, let my stomach grumble and I eat.
Let me be delighted and I laugh.
Let me tire and I rest.
Give my heart peace today
as I am here
surprisingly myself
while the world spins and spins.

---

reflection prompt

I write a lot of sticky notes and put them up to remind my future self of my needs. Otherwise I get overwhelmed. Do you need anything superbasic? Sleep. A snack. Better shampoo. Give yourself permission to have some wonderfully basic responses to the unsolvable problems of the world today. Like, "Okay! I need peanut butter crackers!"

when you're certain that today will be too much

Above all else, guard your heart, for everything you do flows from it.

—PROVERBS 4:23 (NIV)

The ordinariness of our life usually feels like a gift in retrospect. How often have we looked back, in the midst of a crisis, with nostalgia for ordinary days? But when we are *in* an ordinary day and feeling tired and overwhelmed, we can feel frustrated and impatient with ourselves. Shouldn't we have solved these problems already? Shouldn't the whole concept of multitasking have multiplied time somehow? Well, unfortunately no. But God really does love us in our ordinariness. And Jesus spent so much of his time being incredibly ordinary. We have no gospel record of his teenage and young adult life, and scholars speculate that he probably just hung out and worked. See? Spiritual inspiration that we can be regular too. So let's bless our regular problems because, frankly, that's going to be most of life itself.

I was hoping to be
the kind of person by now
who doesn't tumble, headlong,
into the day
falling, falling, falling
from the high board
without nearly enough water below.

God, I swear I didn't plan it like this.
But here I am, hoping for another miracle.

Lord, bless these dumb plans
that will short-circuit my thinking
and make me fragile, brittle.

Lord, bless these multiplying tasks
that swarm like mosquitoes.

Underneath this to-do list
and these calendar invites
and these many obligations
is a set of loves.

Keep love in front of my eyes.
Love in the car.
Love in the waiting room.
Love on the phone.
Love at my laptop.
Love in the laundry room.

And love, especially,
for the soft heart—mine—
who cared enough to be this tired
in the first place.

---

reflection prompt

Try a breath prayer for a regular problem that is irritating you. Think about it (or feel free to just do this breathing prayer in motion while you're dealing with it). You inhale with one thought and exhale with the other. It's very simple, but often effective.

Inhale: Be here.

Exhale: Be here now.

to take what you need

**He makes grass grow
for the cattle,
and plants for people
to cultivate—
bringing forth food
from the earth:
wine that gladdens
human hearts,
oil to make their
faces shine,
and bread that sustains
their hearts.**

—PSALM 104:14-15 (NIV)

Not getting enough sleep? Exhausted from work or kids or parents or just your own unfixable problems? I find that when I am overwhelmed, trying to meet my own needs makes me feel like I'm being selfish. Or I might feel embarrassed and try not to let others know that I'm struggling. Or—and this is very charming—I might loudly declare what I need because now I'm defensive.

But our needs are simply the necessary work of being human. God delights in our humanity, or else God would probably have simply built robots who don't need sleep or poetry or reality television. Read all of Psalm 104 (or even just the verses that start this entry) for a beautiful account of the splendor of what God sets in front of us just to delight us. Creation is reminding us of our own goodness too. Let's take it as a compliment.

The feeder is empty again
and no one is claiming
that the birds are greedy
for taking what they pleased.

Look at how the fat, pink flowers
are weighing the end of each branch,
sucking nutrients into each velvet petal.
How selfish.

Nature hungers, takes, and needs.
God, why can't I?

Blessed are we, learning to take
what we need.
Sleeping past our alarms.
Reaching for another helping.
Staying a little longer
when the evening is unwinding.

Blessed are we, ignoring the rising anxiety
that our needs are somehow silly
because we've survived this long
without the pleasures of this wanting.

God, let these needs be the good sign
of the greening of my life.

---

reflection prompt

*Go outside or look out the window or even
stare at your own houseplant or pet. What can
we learn from their basic needs?*

for finding your truer self again

For God alone my soul waits in silence.

—PSALM 62:1A (NRSVUE)

Sometimes we need to take a step back from the person that our culture is making us. Far too early in life, someone convinced us that we needed to wear a certain brand of clothes. Or live in a certain neighborhood. Or read *this* book and not *that*. We are told that our consumer preferences are part of some grand project of self-expression, but is that really what's happening? I find it a bit horrifying if I glance at my monthly billing statements and wonder, "*WHO AM I?*" Oh boy. This is a blessing for wanting God to be our maker, creator, builder-of-self instead.

God, I am told to invest in myself.
You're worth it.
I should find myself
in the market that owns me.

If you check my billing statements,
I am a monthly subscription
for white noise and sleep stories
and chewable melatonin.

I am a standing grocery order
for dark roast fair-trade beans
and dry, full-bodied Spanish reds.

On a customer-service report somewhere
read aloud in an
air-conditioned boardroom
I represent the value of unlimited
digital access to *The New York Times*
and Wordle. Mostly Wordle.

But, Lord, this is not the creation story
of gardens and mud made flesh,
and life breathed into
one-click ordering.

Unmake me.
Unmake me.
Unmake me.

Put me to sleep.
Steal another rib
and let me awake to all things
astonishingly unnamed and unknown
by the world I made
in affordable monthly installments.

---

reflection prompt

*Imagine yourself far, far away on an island. No
stores. No neighbors. No subscription services.
No tags on any of the clothes you are wearing
(you get comfortable clothes in this scenario!
I'm not cruel!). There is no one there to make
you feel more than or less than anyone else.
You are not winning or losing. You are simply
being. How do you feel? Let's try and take that
sense of self into this day or the next.*

when you don't want to miss someone but you do

I am sick with love.

—SONG OF SOLOMON 2:5B (ESV)

When we loved someone—and I mean love-their-stupid-face-and-miss-their-smell kind of love—that person might pop into our minds at very inconvenient times. They disappointed us. They shouldn't be our forever person. But, regardless, we begin to miss them badly.

The truth is that we carry some form of their love and memory with us. No matter how long it has been since we were together. In fact, we might do a lot of work to never think of them! Good for us! And most of the time it works. But there's a great line in the television show *Crashing* about that lingering feeling.

One character says to another (who she really, actually still loves): "Where does your mind go when it drifts . . ."

This is a blessing for that feeling because, hey, we can bless it and not just tell our friends over the phone. (Also, on pronouns, put them where you need them. Him. Her. Their. Whoever you miss.)

If I heard his voice right now
my heart would start that light jog
toward him
no embarrassment
until I look down to see my shoes
picking up speed.

Or I am sitting in a corner
my knees tucked up
and my arms wrapped around them
watching the feet of passing crowds,
until I hear my name.

God, it's so beautiful how he says it,
and the lurching feeling of how he calls
and I answer.

Funny we should meet like this
(after I've stopped traffic to stand there
in his way).

But if it is very late or very early
or, God, you catch me in a moment
of honesty—
which surprises us both—
I will admit all the ways
I have been formed by his absence,
his failures,
or the way he might have been
something else.
But then he wasn't that at all.

And these disappointments are
stacked up in a pile
that I climb over
when I don't want to be alone.

God, you do not promise a solution
to every kind of loneliness.
After all, you looked down at creation
and made us out of dirt and ribs
in pairs, dammit.
But then we spend so much of our lives
gardening alone.

God, bless those moments when
I wish he were a different kind of person.
And that he had held on
to the mud of my life with both hands.

God, bless the awkwardness,
those texts and letters
which said more, so much more,
about hope
than about what he was willing
or able to do.

And, God, look at my fissured heart
and the unanswered times
when it cries out
without meaning to.
And shout back that it is good,
so absurdly good,
to see my heart beating, so fast and strong,
while you busy yourself
remaking me.

reflection prompt

*Your capacity to love feels like a burden right
now. Think of someone else you love (in any
way, friend, family member, pet, et cetera). And
remind yourself,* Good job. *A lovesick heart is a
heart capable of beautiful things.*

to feel wonder again

The whole earth is filled with awe at your wonders; where morning dawns, where evening fades, you call forth songs of joy.

—PSALM 65:8 (NIV)

I take long walks almost every night to talk to my oldest friend, Chelsea, on the phone. We review the day. We complain. We worry. We encourage. It's a full hour with a real grab bag of feelings. But the moment when I know that we should be genuinely worried about the other person is not when we are riding a roller coaster of emotion. It's when one of us says: "I don't feel much at all." We feel hollow, flat, tired, or discouraged. And walking past house after house, lit up inside and teeming with life, it can be easy to imagine that other people have solved this problem already and never missed a beat.

In moments of dull despair, I pray for wonder. There's a delightful quote by Diane Ackerman that I like to keep nearby, and it reads: "Wonder is the heaviest element on the periodic table. Even a tiny fleck of it stops time." So instead of trying to reach for some of the biggest positive emotions—Happiness! Joy!—I try to get the truth a little sideways by praying for a little fleck of wonder. Maybe you might too.

I stand, stone still,
at the edge of disheartenment.
I have nothing but this certainty:
nothing changes, nothing lasts.
I feel hollow.

God, this world you made is full.
Warm earth pushing up new seedlings,
unfathomable oceans
teeming with mystery,
and the miracle that our clay bodies
bear even the possibility
of creating new life.

We are all swimming in wonder
so, God, why can't I feel it?

I feel my own blood turning cold
with each tiring loss.
Good things, beautiful loves,
pried from my fingers
make them seem empty to me now.

But still.

Even if, today, I am sure
that hope is not knocking at my door,
let the lights at the neighbor's house
glow like a jack-o'-lantern.
Let the sounds,
wafting through the window—

someone's barking dog
and kids running amok,
the buzz of someone's television
rehearsing the day's calamities—
remind me that we persist somehow
under a distant shadow but happy anyway.

Let the sun come down from the sky
and touch me,
and I will walk out to greet it
feeling the low murmur of the ground
beneath my feet.

And as the earth makes its creaky turns
toward night,
let the day fall in behind us.
"What next?" we will say to the night sky,
before we close the door
and consider its answer
tomorrow.

reflection prompt

Let's put aside the big questions of "What next?" today. Allow yourself to settle. Maybe take a few deep breaths. Or allow your mind to dart around until it finds some small detail to notice. A color. A smell. A sensation of any kind. See if it can grow into any sense of wonder.

12

when you need a little motivation to change

I am about to do a new thing; now it springs forth; do you not perceive it? I will make a way in the wilderness and rivers in the desert.

—ISAIAH 43:19 (NRSVUE)

Trying is one of the hardest things in the world, isn't it? I mean, if we want to marvel at just how difficult it is to try, think of something about yourself that you wish was different . . . something you could change if you tried really, really, really hard. (I'll do it too. Okay. I'm thinking of at least three things I wish I could change about myself.) And then, humor me for a moment, but answer the question: How old are you? I'm forty-three. That means I have had at least several decades of *not fixing my stupid problems.* Trying and failing. Not trying and absolutely failing.

If we want to imagine any change, let's give ourselves a small nudge. I will never be the kind of person who imagines everything is possible because, well, most of my problems are unfixable. But if I adopt a theology of small nudges, I can be willing to show up. And as researcher Brené Brown says, "The willingness to show up changes us. It makes us a little braver each time."

I am rummaging through this day
in search of evidence
that tomorrow could be different.

As many times as I wake up
determined to bend the future
with each effort and expectation,
my conviction dissipates by the day's end.

Lord, we are given so few chances
to direct the course of our lives.
So with what little is in my control,
could you help me try?

Let me know the satisfaction of sleep,
exhausted by my effort.
Walk me to the edge of comfort
and keep me there long enough
to reach for something more.

Rescue me from familiar self-hatred.
(You'll never do it. You can't do it.)
Refine my ambition into honest goals.
Quiet my mind when it is already certain
that nothing could possibly be different.
And rekindle a tenderness
in my uncertain heart
for my own small moments of courage
as I peek my head out
from this hiding place
—and all the comfort
of this familiarity—
to announce, "I'M READY!"
if only to myself.

reflection prompt

*Do you feel a small nudge toward anything
today? Even if you've failed to act a million
times before, don't worry about it. Just take a
tiny, tiny step. Whew. We are trying to try! Such
hard work.*

13

when you don't feel fulfilled anymore

A thief comes to steal and kill and destroy, but I came to give life—life in all its fullness.

—JOHN 10:10 (NCV)

I have an overwhelming love of lessons learned from children's books, so today let's take a little encouragement from the great philosopher Dr. Seuss: "Today you are you, that is truer than true. There is no one alive who is you-er than you." We have been launched into this divine experiment called living with all the facets of our particular personalities, families, genetics, traits . . . and God looks on you and smiles. You. You specifically. (Other people are great, but we are not talking about them for a second. YOU ARE A COMPLETE DELIGHT.) When I was trying to explain this to my son when he was four, he nodded knowingly. "Oh yes. God has many, many crushes." Which made me laugh hard.

But we rarely feel that way. So if you need a little encouragement today that you are lovely as yourself and would perhaps like a little divine help getting through the day, this blessing is for you.

God, I will wake up today and move,
numbly,
into each new hour.

I will fill my lungs with the air
of an undone, unfinished,
never-before-seen day,
entirely certain of how I will feel
when it ends:
tired.
bored.
unchanged.

God, even my best efforts—
my sacrificial love, my diligent work—
don't stir up anything
like the rush of accomplishment.

Whatever felt like meaning
isn't meaningful anymore.
At least not today.

One minute, I want to change everything.
And the next I want to crawl back into bed.
(But, if I'm honest, how much of my actual
day-to-day life could I change,
even if I wanted to?)

Lord, this is the simplest prayer:
make it matter again.
Color my grayscale vision
with every shade of meaning.
Blues and purples and lilacs for purpose.
Reds and pinks for every kind of love.
Yellows for insights and ideas that sparkle.

And if once-cherished dreams need to fade,
let them fade.
Let me not imagine
that each one of my plans
must glue my future together.

Surprise me.
(I regret saying that already.)
But let me come alive to the wonder
of this day.

reflection prompt

Try this prayer for today in whatever you are doing: "Lord, make this matter."

to stop trying to fix everything

There is a story in the gospel of Luke where Jesus visits the home of Mary and Martha. Martha is running around trying to finish all the hospitality work for having Jesus and all his disciples, who were likely needing things, eating things, asking about where to sit. And Martha whips around only to see her sister, Mary, *not doing anything.* She's just sitting there listening to Jesus. Honestly, I am on Team Martha here (please get up and help, sibling of mine), but Jesus tells Martha to cool it. (See scripture at the beginning of this entry.)

I have an incredibly vivid memory of walking in on my little sister, Maria, working in a frenzy. She had flour on her face and all over her dress. She was carrying at least four objects with no useful relationship to each other: an apron, a silver mixing bowl of confetti, a black music stand, and a single egg. And she said, without missing a beat, "I'm having a lot of Martha feelings right now." Hysterical. Give this woman a Netflix series.

Many of us are caregivers and looking out for the needs of others. It can be really difficult to turn down the volume of other people's needs. Let's calm our hypervigilant hearts for a moment.

God, I know how to worry.
I've trained my whole body to leap
headlong, heart-forward
into the future.

Is someone thinking about
everyone's dinner yet?
HOLD ON TIGHT.
ENGAGING WARP SPEED.
I'LL BE RIGHT THERE.

When I'm doing it, God,
it's not called worry.
It's *anticipation*.
No, it's *thoughtfulness*.
Generosity even.

I feel its pull in the moment
before fully waking.
Before I open my eyes, Lord,
I can see the needs of the day
like trees littering summer leaves
all over the lawn.

Give me a second, God, to imagine it:
peace.

A cup of coffee in my hands,
a spreading calm in my chest,
the creeping knowledge that you,
at the edges of my mind,
are hemming me in.

Lord, slow my hands,
twitchy between tasks.
Bolt my feet to the ground
if you must.
Untie me from my conviction that
only *good Christians* are this tired,
this jumpy, this hamstrung by the future.

God, save me from all my best qualities.
I am drowning in them.

---

reflection prompt

*Let's consider the hilarious wisdom of the
wizard Gandalf from J.R.R. Tolkien's treasured
Lord of the Rings books. He too had decided
that enough was enough: "I must rest here a
moment, even if all the orcs ever spawned are
after us." What orcs are after you right now?
Do you still need to rest anyhow?*

for a terrible day

**Fearfulness and
trembling have come
upon me,
And horror has
overwhelmed me.**

—PSALM 55:5 (NKJV)

One of the most defining features of tragedy is the way that time feels. Its slowness. Its surrealness. The "is this really happening?" feeling. T. H. White, an author who knew much suffering, described tragedy as that feeling when, it seems, "innocence is not enough." The bad thing is happening to you regardless. So, first of all, permit me to say that I'm so sorry that you are having this kind of day. Let's just pray for you right now, shall we?

That tick, tick, tick
of an ordinary day whirring along.
Where is it now?
Time has slowed to a stop,
yet this growing feeling of dread
races through my thoughts
and seeps into my heart.
A dark ink clouding
every clear, clear thought
makes me certain, all at once,
that this will never end.
(That's how it feels, at least.)

Even the shock of it—
pupils widening, pinpricked skin,
the gallop of my pulse
when I turn my face toward it—
is not fading.

Lord, there will be few solutions today.
Few answers to dig out and hold up to you
saying, "See? Will this work?"
So slow my quickened mind.
Hurry others to notice my distress.

Sing me silently into lulling peace
beyond my manufacturing.
Slough off whatever can be shed
and fill my heart, now starved of hope,
with the great comfort that
wherever you are, in heaven and on earth,
tucked behind those clouds
or someone's eyes,
that you, hour by hour,
will rescue me from this day.
I'll close my eyes now and wait as you
deliver me safely through the dusk.

---

reflection prompt

*In a moment like this, the breath God gave us
can work for us. So try to address the panic a
little and slow down to the pace of your chest
rising and falling.*

Breathe in slowly:

1...2...3...

Now breathe out even slower:

1...2...3...4...

*Repeat until you feel your shoulders drop a
little and your heart rate slows.*

when you need a break

Your mind will be clear, free from fear; when you lie down to rest, you will be refreshed by sweet sleep.

—PROVERBS 3:24 (VOICE)

We come from a "fix-it" culture. But there's no outworking the sheer reality of our fatigue. You might be feeling incredibly tired. Maybe you feel embarrassed that you really can't do it all.

I grew up in southern Manitoba around a religious group called the Mennonites. What people normally associate with Mennonites is their commitment to pacifism and simplicity. But, sweet mercy, their most defining feature is their industriousness. You cannot tear them away from an unopened box of IKEA furniture. (Unfinished work lies there like it's taunting them.) I always thought it was very funny that they have such a cute word in Low German (the mother tongue of many Mennonites) for the term *little nap*. The word is *meddachschlop*. Adorable. Except I swear to you I have never seen a Mennonite take a little nap.

But that's often how it is. We have words in our vocabulary that we never actually put into practice. Words like *rest* or *Sabbath* or, if you are my father-in-law, *meddachschlop*. Let's bless the need we might have to take it down a notch.

God, my body is telling me things
I'm having a hard time hearing
amid the noise of so many pressing needs.

They shout loudly
about the world melting into plastic
(*hadn't you noticed?*)
and hadn't you better get on with doing
something about it?

Most days I'd be up in a second
looking for my bucket,
ready to douse these flames.

But not today.
Today is not most days.

Today is the day I begin to notice
my body slowing,
tensing, bracing.

It is tugging at the edges
of my whirring thoughts
asking to be heard.

I have confused fatigue with weakness,
finitude with lack of self-mastery.
I am dragged into my humanity,
kicking and screaming,
but fine.

Clear the smoke, God,
so I can feel the naturalness of
rest and peace and renewal.
There.
Lift me back onto my feet,
but only when I'm ready
to set out
to love others once again.

---

reflection prompt

Schedule a meddachschlop *in your calendar. I dare you. Consider it a helpful lesson for Mennonites everywhere (including me).*

when you need to forgive

Forgive others, and you will
be forgiven.

—LUKE 6:37B (NLT)

Over the course of our lives, we might see a miracle. We might see something that entirely defies explanation. God has worked against the laws of nature to heal or rescue or transform, and we can only pause in wonder.

People talk a lot about forgiveness (such an ordinary word!), but I really do believe that real forgiveness is a miracle. When was the last time you saw forgiveness that defied explanation? The person who was wronged didn't seem bitter or wounded, but somehow whole? Incredible. Unbelievable. Wow.

The more common reality is that we are angry, we are hurt, we are fearful. We are pissed, we are annoyed, and we are rehearsing exactly what we would say to them. They were wrong, and the pain they caused has taken root in us. We might feel absolute hatred. Fair.

Even so, we need forgiveness in our lives. We need forgiveness because, as the priest and theologian Henri Nouwen observed, we love poorly too. He writes: "The hard truth is that all people love poorly. We need to forgive and be forgiven every day, every hour increasingly. That is the great work of love among the fellowship of the weak that is the human family."

I have come to see forgiveness as a rare and beautiful thing. It's the miracle we need every day. It is something we can pray for and take steps toward, but don't be hard on yourself if this is complicated terrain. We can simply pray: *Lord, protect me and change me all at once. You are making me a miracle.*

We are trapped, Lord,
in this world of shadows.
We stand over reservoirs, cracked and dry,
familiar with the emptiness
that confirms something in us:
nothing grows here.

Love. Forgiveness. Reconciliation.
It would be easier to imagine
the suspension of the laws of nature,
gravity moving up instead of down,
our feet suddenly suspended
above this dust,
than imagine anything beautiful
after everything that's happened.
Everything they've said.
Everything they've done.
Impossible.
We bristle at even the thought
of this place renewed,
the trickle of water, the return of birdsong,
waters bubbling up from the deep.
The restoration of our souls.

Lord, it is not a failure of our imagination.
The world runs on cause and effect.
Eye for an eye and the righteous assurances
of the newly blind.
Why, why, why put yourself out there?
Protect yourself. They don't deserve you.

They're right.
This kind of love would be beyond reason.
If you were to do something, anything,
after all of this,
it would take a miracle.

Jesus, you place forgiveness at the center
of the healing of the world.
Somehow you could murmur
"forgive them" to your enemies
and comfort to your friends
even before the undoing of evil
in the resurrection was in view.
But you look at every shadowed place,
every empty heart and brittle hope,
and plant in us a seed of wonder.
Could something new grow here
amidst the rot and ruin?
Something that safeguards our hearts
and risks them, all at once.
Restore us. Renew us.
Begin where nothing grows.

---

reflection prompt

Let's try a gentle prayer of forgiveness. Perhaps
someone comes to mind that we would like to
forgive. Maybe we could say: "Lord, protect me
and change me as I seek to forgive."

when someone has done you harm

Blessed be the Lord, my rock, who trains my hands for war and my fingers for battle.

—PSALM 144:1 (NRSVUE)

You are worthy of being protected. In case you haven't heard that lately, really, you deserve big thick boundaries that protect you. In the aftermath of a terrible thing done to you, it can be difficult to remember that you are worthy of all manner of love, safety, and people who stand up for you.

Many of us have not experienced that kind of safety in spiritual communities. Perhaps we have witnessed the church acting in bad faith. We may have seen people we love (or been the person) guilted and manipulated into silence or "forgiveness" instead of being able to say: "This person did me harm."

If you have experienced a breach of trust or someone who has done you wrong, let's allow ourselves the spiritual words for rage and lament and whatever is ours to name.

God, there is a long list of possible terrors
crowding every newspaper.
But there is a kind of terror, Lord,
for which I am unprepared.
Someone cannot be trusted.

A spiritual world of
forgive, forgive, forgive
made me a lamb.

I learned to take down every fence
that kept me from harm.
I needed barbed wire,
not lions left to graze.

I might have been angry
if I had thought it was permitted.
I might have been wary if I had
allowed myself to take note.
How was I?
Nervous, queasy, worried, and, worst of all,
quieted with a misplaced shame.

Lord, restore in me a deep,
immovable trust
that I have language for evil—those
behaviors, intentions, and even
institutions that are willfully
determined to engineer my harm.

You gave me eyes—now help me see.

Make me nimble in discernment
and ruthless in truth.
Whatever and whoever seeks
to tarnish and gaslight,
tear down and consume
for its own purposes,
let it be dragged into the great bonfire
that is your light.

I am a lamb, yes.
But you are the great shepherd
who promised something so strange.
When you see the flock crowded together,
safe and snug,
—except one, except me—
you will not rest.
You will rescue me.

reflection prompt

*Perhaps there is a vulnerability within you that
needs protecting. If it feels too tender to look at
right now, tuck it away until the time is right to
think about it or share. But in all things—easy
or impossible—you have every right to call on
God as your witness and great ally.*

quieting an anxious mind

In every situation, by prayer and petition, with thanksgiving, present your requests to God. And the peace of God, which transcends all understanding, will guard your hearts and your minds in Christ Jesus.

—PHILIPPIANS 4:6-7 (NIV)

Trying to quiet an anxious mind is like drawing a circle over a circle over a circle. Every instruction to be calm stirs up another thought, and then another. We worry and then, to solve it, we worry about worrying. And this entry's scripture from the letter to the Philippians can be a bit daunting. Can we really find peace if we bring *every situation* to God? And if I worry, does that mean I'm not praying right? Or am not spiritual enough?

Instead of berating ourselves for not being worry-free, let's imagine for a moment that peace is like a homecoming. We are at the end of a story and it's time to return home to rest. We are like Peter Rabbit coming back to his cozy burrow when he's done a day of racing around Mr. McGregor's garden. (See how much I love children's books? Sigh. They are like a weighted blanket.) When we cannot solve the problem of our worried minds, let's bless our desire to return home to ourselves. We are very tired rabbits indeed.

If I close my eyes, God,
I will only feel the current of each worry—
every undone action,
every unresolved hope,
every unfinished argument churning up
emotion after emotion.
I am bracing against my own mind
as each thought spins around and around.

I am spent. Uneasy and heartsore.
Let me slow my work,
my thoughts, to a trickle.
Pour them out, Lord,
and let them slide away
like a barely remembered dream.
When I reach for thoughts that push me—
one way or another—
let them evaporate in my hands.

Lord, even you rested.
Even you gave yourself over to stillness
and, like a pool of clear water,
allowed peace to uncloud
every gray sorrow.

Every breath is your own making, God.
In and out.
In and out.
Fill me with surprising calm.
Fill me with the gentle nothingness
of your quieting love.

reflection prompt

Hand on your heart. Let your mind spin without chastising it. Pat your heart in a nice slow rhythm. There you are. Home at last.

for everyday funerals

The grass withers and the flowers fall, but the word of the Lord endures forever.

—1 PETER 1:24B-25A (NIV)

Now that I know a bit more about grief in my own life, I notice endings everywhere. Some are actual burials. Some are simply the knowledge that something lovely is over. We have so many rituals for our big moments (weddings! graduations!) and so few for the moments of heartbreak. But those are the reminders of, as Rabbi Steve Leder says, the beauty of what remains. So here's a blessing for funerals—everyday funerals—big and small. May we feel the weight of our loves. Every act of love is a heartbreaker, we know that now.

When archaeologists dig down deep
in the hard-packed sediment
of civilizations
come and gone
they find flowers, dried flowers,
strewn among the bones.
Someone was laid down
among their people
and the first thought,
the best thought,
was to pull flowers from the dirt
to accompany them.

We know an ending when we see one.

We attend funerals every day.
Big and small,
we see our endings.
Last day of school, last hope in that friend,
end of this love or that bit of youth.
Last touch of their warm,
paper-skinned hand
before they are stolen away
to braid grass into crowns
with the King of Heaven.

And if we are lucky, so very lucky,
we pause once a day.
We feel a kindling in our heart
which reminds us:
there it is and there it goes.
We tilt our heads, then glance back,
fast enough to see it fade.
And we feel the magnitude
of such a miracle—
that anything, anyone, began at all.
And we find ourselves,
hearts weighed down by too much love,
pulling at the grass,
searching for flowers.

reflection prompt

We are promised by God that some things will last forever. Christians believe, against all evidence, that we will live forever with God after we die. (We go big! We can say that about ourselves.) But let's take a second to think of something, big or small, that is gone. An ability you had. A friend who is gone. Remember the first moment you knew it was ever yours at all and thank God.

for whatever is on the calendar

And whoever gives one of these little ones even a cup of cold water because he is a disciple, truly, I say to you, he will by no means lose his reward.

—MATTHEW 10:42 (ESV)

Every time I do something really difficult, I make an award chart. I know it is completely ridiculous. Truly. It's so dumb. But picture me attempting to get a doctoral degree from a fancy university with a lot of stone gargoyles and leather-bound books. But then I needed to read about 350 of those leather-bound books in a short period of time, so what did I do? I made an enormous chart with a point system. Three points for a book I had never read! Two points for a difficult article in a journal! One point if I could simply recite the argument without having finished the book! And then I bought reams of stickers shaped like stars and made each point a star. If I could have done something similar with chemotherapy when I was diagnosed with cancer, I would have. When life is hard, I secretly wish someone out there is keeping score and clapping.

I wish you could get an award for everything you do for others. I would build the podium myself. We could have a whole point system. Made a horrible appointment? Two stars! Loved an enemy? Three stars!

But instead, most of the difficult and painful choices we make to love others and get up again after being knocked down will have no audience. No clapping. At most, we will get a small sense that we are moving in the right direction. So today let's consider the things we do and what they cost, even though we probably won't get a medal for whatever happens.

I will admit, God, that I am hoping
there will be an award ceremony.
Nothing fancy.
But my name will be called from a podium
and I will, hand fluttering to my heart
in feigned surprise,
rise to speak, saying a few words of thanks
for this great honor:
I did everything on the calendar this week.

I attended meetings bookended
with at least five minutes of small talk.
I went to appointments that
gobbled up my money.
(*Don't forget to schedule a follow-up on
your way out.*)
I ran errands to solve problems that loved
ones will probably never realize they had.
I checked on people
who don't check on me.

Lord, love is a chore.

But then, Holy Spirit,
you were there somehow
when I had to shampoo the dog
and someone else couldn't find
their medication.
You were decidedly *not there*
when I was in traffic,

but by the time I'd arrived,
I felt that familiar tug
of your insistence on tending to the people
who would need me
when I got out of the car.

Lord, most of the time I am consumed
by my own resentments
at how exhausting, annoying,
and soul-depleting
it feels to be indispensable.
Then the guilt—oh, the guilt—
at not cheering at every act of service.

So, Lord, let me hear you say it:
"Well done, good and faithful one.
You did what was on the calendar."
And now draw me into your arms
with a few extra assurances
that you adore me equally
when I do nothing, nothing, nothing at all.

---

reflection prompt
*Let's award ourselves some Invisibility Points
that God really does notice. Did we try
anyway? Did we accept a bit of rest? God is
there, keeping score and clapping.*

for when things are falling apart

**I called on your name, Lord,
Out of the lowest pit.**

—LAMENTATIONS 3:55 (NASB)

There is a tradition of lament that weaves through scripture like a black thread. These scriptures demand to know where God has gone. They cry out with pain in times of absolute despair. They demand vengeance and help and someone to hear how quickly, how quickly, how quickly our lives can fall apart. It's a normal day and then, *whoosh,* a storm comes rushing in. When the rain is hammering at our windows and the waters are rising, I don't need an elaborate prayer. I don't need long, impressive doctrinal statements about God or the state of the world. I need honesty. I need help. And I need courage.

If there is a storm in your life, I hope you feel the righteousness of your own prayers when you say: *God, hear me. God, save me. God, grant me courage*. Here is a blessing for before the storm has passed.

I am a house built too close
to the shore, God,
and the storm has come.

I can hear the wood splintering.
The wind is tearing at my bones.
What will be left?

Long ago, I had drawn up the blueprints
with a steady hand and
a heart full of hope.
It took painstaking efforts to build
this life, these years, this day—
the one being ripped,
plank by plank,
to the studs.

Tragedy is so casual, isn't it?
What it takes and what it leaves.

I am paper and glue
and thumbtacks and photos
hung by a string
of each good, good love I shelter.

Lord, you promised me
the gift of your spirit and living waters
and everlasting life.
You promised me your son, Jesus Christ,
with me now and forever,
and the fellowship of the Triune God
and the sweetness of heaven.

But, God, give me back today.
Slow these winds and still my racing heart.
Shelter me, help me, save me.
Hold my life together, Lord,
while the storms are raging on.

reflection prompt

*You may have been raised in a spiritual
tradition that preferred that you have a lot of
polite spiritual feelings. "Dear God, if you're not
too busy . . ." Feel free to bring any untidy
prayers to God's attention. God is yours to call
upon. Not just someone else's who has it all
together.*

a blessing for a good pause

Be still, and know that I am God.

—PSALM 46:10A (NIV)

Emily Dickinson, the nineteenth-century poet of solitude, knew the beauty of stillness. She described that moment of pause as the deepest kind of privacy when a soul is admitted into its own company. It feels like "finite infinity," she concluded.

That kind of quiet feels elusive to us. We ache to know our souls' calm, but also, isn't there something on Netflix? Wait, let me check my texts first. Before we know it, we are swimming around in a sea of notifications and updates without direction. Nothing is more precious than our attention, but we give it away without knowing its cost. I mean, who can blame us? We are living in an attention economy where the first casualty is peace, peace, peace. So let's bless our distracted selves. If we can't bring ourselves to desire stillness, maybe we can talk ourselves into wanting a little less noise.

This is the moment. I can feel it.

It is the microsecond pause

before the habitual override

that sends me into motion again.

Barreling ahead instead of paying attention

to what my body is trying to tell me

about its limitations,

to what pulls on my mind,

to your spirit's wisdom, so hard won.

I'm here, now, in the blessed in-between,

the transition phase that isn't anything yet.

It's a pivot point that would be a shame

to waste again,

with mindless scrolling

or what is happening in the news?

Right.

Stop.

Stay.

This is the sacred space of the nothing-yet,

a place where I can become aware

that you are pulling at me, tugging at me.

Be present with me here,

in these whirring seconds,

at the tiny crossroads that is this moment,

slowing me long enough to wonder:

Is that you tapping me on the shoulder?

All right. I'm listening.

---

reflection prompt

*Turn off your phone. Close the door. Be quiet
for five minutes. See if you can settle into
wanting to turn toward God's love.*

when you have screwed up

How does it feel when you are wrong? Do you feel flushed or embarrassed? Angry or defensive? Do you ignore the mistake altogether and hope to make it up gradually without bringing it up again? My preferred avoidance strategy is to call a friend in hopes that he or she will explain away my mistake. "It wasn't so bad!" *Oh, wait. Maybe it was.*

Learning to be wrong is difficult and complicated work. We do not want to learn the habit of feeling unnecessarily guilty (many of us feel that way already!). And we do not want stewing in the consequences to keep us from the work of repair. We need a God who already loves us to show us how to be *the right amount of wrong.* (Also, how is that not a country music song already? I would buy anything called "The Right Amount of Wrong.") We have a forgiving God who wants us to admit our wrongdoing . . . because, even before we do, God is busy yelling, *I LOVE YOU ANYWAY.* Let's take a minute to take a gentle inventory of something we may need to correct.

It would be easier, right now,
to call someone who loves me
with a delightful, delusional love
so I can hear them say: "It wasn't you.
You didn't know.
It was an honest mistake."

But sometimes, Lord, I knew.

God, I have this feeling of unrest,
and peace has slipped away.
I know that somewhere in this mess
is a wrong I chose.

Lord, don't let me hide in my shame.
Keep it from wrapping me up
with half-truths.
I have let someone down, even myself,
and I can't yet separate out all the threads
of my knotted-up heart.

There is something familiar about it,
and that makes me even more
upset with myself.
I've done this before I think,
but I can barely let myself say
that a second time.
Is this me?
I don't want to wear it,
so I'm keeping it at arm's length.

But that is actually untenable—
this shame, this worry, this heartsick fear.
I can't be okay about this
until I'm clear about what happened
and what to do about it.

God, show me the whole truth of it,
in every aspect of its unfolding.
The missteps, and the decisions
that directed them.

This is medicine. Strong medicine.
Here to heal me.
Here to heal the world I love.
And I swear,
tomorrow (just give me a minute, Lord)
I will act as one being nursed to health
as you restore me to myself.

reflection prompt

*Does a particular mistake come to mind?
Consider a little step toward . . . you know . . .
being wrong. Have you admitted it to yourself?
Have you said it out loud to them? Think about
a small, lovely thing you might do, even if it is
just saying to yourself, "I'm really going to get
more comfortable with being sorry."*

when life feels out of control

For I am convinced that neither death nor life, neither angels nor demons, neither the present nor the future, nor any powers, neither height nor depth, nor anything else in all creation, will be able to separate us from the love of God that is in Christ Jesus our Lord.

—ROMANS 8:38-39 (NIV)

Sometimes when we say "I feel like my life is out of control," the sanest thing to do is admit that. Maybe your life is genuinely out of control. Sometimes we have few choices, if any. So let's take a minute and breathe. Let's repeat the promises of this beautiful refrain in Paul's letter to the Romans. Now, when you feel like you are spinning, can you be separated from God's love? No. Nothing can separate you. Not death nor life. Not angels nor demons. Not the present, not the future. No powers that rule. Nothing in creation. You are in the very center of God's love. Promise.

There was a time when
I had a grip on things,
and a few decent plans.
Even a theory or two about
how to keep my balance
on this spinning planet.

And then.
And then.
And then.

Life shook me loose.
I blinked only to find myself hurtling
through time,
through a darkness I couldn't fathom
(but surely, it must have been there
all along),
the truth echoing in my ears:

    we come undone.

      things fall.

        gravity itself fails.

At this speed, well-intentioned invitations
to stop and smell the roses
or welcome the surprises of the day
sound dainty. Charming even.
Belonging to another place and time.

They can't reach me.

I am throwing an anchor
out into the ether
and, Lord, will you catch it?
Grab it. Tether it.
Pull me into your orbit.

Let my eyes adjust and absorb
the truth of the beautiful, terrible world
you made and we share
with the people we love.

When I feel the ground pitching
and my stomach lurching,
convince me, once again,
that the vastness of this universe
is a comfort to me, somehow.
No matter how tiny my place
in infinite space,
I will stay at the center of your love.

---

reflection prompt

*From beyond the vastness of the cosmos that
began billions of years ago, it was decided.
You're loved. It is one of the strangest parts of
being loved by a God who exists inside and
outside of time. We have been pulled into that
orbit of love that knows no end, where
everywhere can be the center, even where you
sit right now. Take a minute to put yourself in
the center of God's story. Honestly, you're
allowed.*

to enjoy the fullness of the day

Consider the lilies of the field, how they grow; they toil not, neither do they spin; And yet I say unto you, That even Solomon in all his glory was not arrayed like one of these.

—MATTHEW 6:28B-29 (KJV)

There's a lot of pressure nowadays to live in the moment. WOULDN'T THAT BE NICE. It's a very "consider the lilies" mindset when we can stay in the present without skipping to the future or drifting back to the past.

The truth is that sometimes enjoying the fullness of the day feels easy and sometimes it feels impossible. Perhaps the speed of your life is set to hyperdrive. Perhaps the burdens you are carrying make it painful to live in the moment. When I was in the thick of chemotherapy, I wanted to do anything but live in the present . . . the present was fluorescent lights and sticky floors and bloodwork. So let's be wonderfully realistic and try to carve out a little possibility in whatever day or night we're having.

This bounded space that is today
is the gift I gently hold with my two hands,
like a familiar, cherished face.

Oh, God, let my thoughts be kind
as my mind sweeps over the hours
in front of me.

The sights and sounds of all
who will greet me,
my ridiculous, favorite people.
The sound of each voice and sigh.
That shoulder slouch, that grin.
Let me squirrel every image away
as a treasured possibility.

It's a little trick I learned when I am sad.
Steal from the future
and make it mine now.
All I have to do is feel
every imaginable love
to close the gap between time and space.

Look, if I don't keep my gaze soft
I will probably notice all this laundry.
I will remember that there were
thirty-four tasks
already promised and undelivered.

But I see and hold it all now,
as if my life had been cleaned, polished,
then suddenly returned to me.

Lord, fill me with happiness
because these hours and minutes
are so inconceivably,
astonishingly precious.

And as I begin the day,
translate all things ordinary
and commonplace,
stupid or boring, funny or profound,
into yet another reminder
that each is somehow shimmering.

reflection prompt
*Look at where the light has fallen in the room.
The sunlight. The fluorescent bulb. Wherever
you are, chaotic or calm, look again at the light
and the shadows. Notice anything, anything,
anything that strikes you as beautiful. And be
happy for a second, just because.*

you're being too productive

My grace is sufficient for you, for my power is made perfect in weakness.

—2 CORINTHIANS 12:9 (NIV)

I hate to work against myself here and draw your attention to this fact but, look, you could be doing work right now. And you're not. You're reading this. Or perhaps you have become confused and believe that reading this devotional is actually productive. I often confuse doing something spiritual with doing something productive, so I should probably remind us both that it's much more likely that Christianity is going to make your life less efficient. I will never forget a sermon I heard from my friend Tim Conder, who had a congregation of mostly students, and he gave a barn-burning sermon one Sunday about how our faith would likely make our lives measurably worse. We would have to begin rooting for the losing team. We would have to begin to give away more money and more time. God would start speaking to us in the silence when we weren't racing to the next thing.

If you need to simmer down a little, take it down a notch, become less buzzy, this blessing is for you. And if you really, really don't want to become less efficient, then this blessing is *definitely* for you. We don't usually want the medicine that cures us. But we have a God who loves to hold us, calm us, and reorient us. Let's see what happens when we do.

God, it's time to call it.
My productivity is out of control.
I'm filling every second with the task
that will make the next one work.
And even my downtimes are planned
so far in advance
they can't anticipate what life
will actually look like.

Oh, but the *joy of knocking out*
a gazillion tasks!
Who will let me be triumphant
about that!
I thrill at the hum of
racing around the bases and
sliding feetfirst into the next one.

Am I made to do this?
Or have I crossed a line
and started to let this gift govern me?

God, slow me. This thrumming
in my heart tells me
I will resist you.
But I really do want to know
what beautiful things surface
between breaths.

What I call inefficiency do you call rest?
What I consider time-wasting
is likely another path to a virtue
I cannot define
as I speed blearily to the finish.

God, make me fruitfully,
horrifyingly unproductive.
Astonish me with an unfamiliar
speed of love.

---

reflection prompt

Look at us, not working. You did it. Two minutes
of in-between. Of possibility. If you're one for
the box-ticking, heart-racing thrill of
accomplishment, consider this: What if the in-
between is the pivot point you need most? I'm
going to call that pivot point "unwork" because
it's so unfamiliar and strange to us productive
types. Let's do some unwork today. I'm
convinced it will free us up to move at the
speed of love.

when you are in pain

**Hear my prayer, Lord;
let my cry for help come
to you.**

—PSALM 102:1 (NIV)

There are days, weeks, even years where we might feel lost to pain. The world becomes small and barely manageable and, worst of all, boring in a tragic sort of way. We might feel like we are out of options or we have used up the goodwill of others. It is like someone has painted over our future in greasy black paint.

I have found that pain—mine or someone else's—is an incredible amount of work because none of the solutions are obvious. Suffering is the pain that endures, so we have often already exhausted our best ideas. We may need to ask God for a supernatural sense of curiosity to return to fundamental questions: What works? What else can I try? Who can I ask? So here is a blessing for a painful day, a blessing to shoo away any despair. Even on days when you feel lost to yourself, God is there to find you.

I only have a minute, God,

before the pain rushes in so speedily

that it will wash me away.

Did I have a personality before? Hobbies?

I sound like I was an interesting person...

Lord, pain has come to live with me

and there isn't room for both of us.

It stops me when I move.

It intrudes on my best thoughts.

It crowds the day

with its ragged necessities.

It robs me when I sleep

of hope I tucked away for tomorrow.

And look, God, how it steals from others.

It's not just me.

There is an ache I can see

in the eyes of friends and family

before they hide it in their love.

God, we are exhausted from

all this heavy lifting.

Look, we are on borrowed energy here.

So I will pray as honestly and plainly

as I know how:

God, please send help.

Make the pain subside.

Remind me of the good questions lurking

here somewhere:

> Is there something new to try?

> Who else can help me?

> What old solution could be recycled?

> What am I missing?

And in the meantime, give me the strength

for what I cannot avoid,

but once it's done, Lord, tuck me in.

I'm spent.

reflection prompt

The author C. S. Lewis was an astute observer of the loudness of pain when he described it as insistent, *far more insistent than any pleasure. So let's try shouting something back. We can pray for insistent help. We can ask someone else for help. Or we can just yell, "C'MON, LOVIE! LET'S SEE WHAT WORKS!" if only to ourselves. Because we are usually pretty wise and are about to come up with something new.*

when you judge everyone

Do not be overcome by evil, but overcome evil with good.

—ROMANS 12:21 (NIV)

It will be no surprise to you when I say that we are living in a historical moment of very little compassion for other people's politics. We are drowning in our disgust for others. (At least I am at times. Watch my eyes when I read a bumper sticker I find offensive. It looks like I've been doused in gasoline.)

I learned a beautiful lesson from a nurse named Christie Watson about what it takes to overcome feelings of judgment. Nurses don't ask if the patient tried to prevent the illness that brought them into the hospital. They don't wonder aloud if the patient's sickness puts their own health at risk. Instead, they must cultivate tremendous empathy as they tend to the sick and suffering regardless of who they are or what they have done. What if it is easy to judge? One nurse responded, quoting Mother Teresa, "If you judge people, you have no time to love them." Whew. May we find little time to judge people today because we are so terribly busy loving them.

Kids are mucking about on the playground
but why hasn't anyone asked
who they voted for?
Someone needs to tell them
that they should already know
what to think and who to listen to
and whether they deserve compassion
if they fall and cry and bleed.

Lord, I want to love what is good
and act justly and love mercy
and walk humbly and whatnot.
But every soft opinion I've ever had
has been calcified into
someone else's certainty.
All our bones are on the outside now.

Save me from disdain and disgust
and algorithms
that sort all my friends into demographics.
Spur me to swift action when I see
broken systems that break people
for profit.

Quicken my rage when it directs
my best efforts,
but never, ever let me forget that,
Lord, our deepest story is love.

As I inventory others with
ruthless efficiency,
sorting through their many, *obvious* faults,
let me pause.
Remind me again
how we were kids
not so long ago
before I forged my heart with iron.

---

reflection prompt

There's a reason judges sit on high benches. Their height is a symbol of the fact that they preside over proceedings and determine outcomes. We have no such role in our everyday lives, but we do have the capacity to discern. What if we turned our observations into discernment? The kind that steps back from the drama and reflects on it with the compassion we ourselves would love to receive. Allow a judgment to pop into your mind and see if you can transform it into a softer hope for others.

for married love

**Iron sharpens iron,
and one person sharpens
another.**
—PROVERBS 27:17 (CSB)

One of the funniest things about meeting people who have been married for a long time is how quickly they will tell you about it.

Me: Oh, nice to meet you! What's your name?

Them: I HAVE BEEN WITH LINDA FOR FORTY-FIVE YEARS!

Me: What did you say you do for work?

Them: FORTY-FIVE YEARS!

Marriage is one of the most difficult and most rewarding commitments that we make. We make promises to someone long before we know if we have the ability or willingness to follow through. We get up in front of witnesses and declare that love conquers all even when, at some point, we may feel entirely conquered by other circumstances instead. It's as if we peer into the future and, instead of seeing nothing much at all, decide that we see ourselves there, older, changed, and loved. That takes such courage, such hope.

However we have experienced marriage—as a refuge (or not), a partnership (or not)—I wonder if we could bless it. Unconditional love is rare. When we see it in ourselves or anyone else, let's draw close to it like we are warming ourselves by a fire. We are learning something about God's long covenants of love.

Lord, thank you for the love that endures.
Love that rings on
long after the note is struck.
Love that holds together two
who solemnly swear
to be faithful to one another
without even a reasonable foreshadowing
of what the world will bring
to their doorstep.

Begun in hope,
witnessed and celebrated in community,
and blessed by God.
We promise and you promise.
That's why it's sacred.
We hold on to what holds us.

Of all endeavors it is the
most awe-inspiring
and the hardest to fulfill.
For it's only after the wedding
that the marriage can begin.
After the promises are made
and the vows sealed
then—*poof*—a wife or a husband appears.
(*Who is that?!*)
And the best and worst in each.

Blessed are we who become
witnesses to the truth
that every person is a foreign country,
even to themselves.
Marriage must therefore be an unveiling
at the borderline where desires meet,
in confluence or in conflict,
and sharp corners chafe
and are rubbed smooth,
proof that the whole is greater
than the sum of the parts.

Blessed are we in celebration
of married love,
where in one word or a glance,
an old joke can be fully reconstituted,
no footnotes required.
You know it's a miracle when we set aside
our predictable self-sabotage
for a love that brings us back to each other.

---

reflection prompt

*Can you think of an annoying quality or quirk
you have that has been tempered by someone
else's love? (I never close cupboard doors.
Never. Everything is open, as the Lord
intended.) Let's thank God for the people who
change us.*

when life feels incomplete

Hope deferred makes the heart sick, but a desire fulfilled is a tree of life.

—PROVERBS 13:12 (ESV)

I always imagined that, if I was faithful and good, I would stop feeling the ache of want. I would refine my ambitions and sanctify my desires and then I would feel full. Surely that is the benefit of being a Christian? A self-satisfied expression of total bliss?

Perhaps it is more honest to admit that we were born hungry and the hunger doesn't stop as the years go by. Let's consider that for a moment, letting ourselves do a light inventory of what makes us feel hungry and incomplete. Are we in want of a different kind of friendship or love? Is it a new kind of dream or ambition? Is it release from an addiction or a cycle that hems us in? Where are our hungers pointing us today?

When the shoes are all over the floor,
and the laundry is growing mildew,
I stare.
The facts of my life are strewn everywhere.
This is it.
These are the choices I made,
and the ones made for me.

Friends might congratulate me
on some well-chosen loves,
sacrifices I made for a good, good thing.
A job or a partner, friends or a parent,
didn't I follow my heart and consult
my better angels?
But here I am.
Incomplete somehow.

Lord, sometimes my emptiness
is ringing with a name.
He is gone. She is somewhere else.
Wouldn't I be full again
if only, if only, if only?

I would starve if I could let myself hunger.
But instead I check email and run errands.
I am playing checkers with my life
and the world is playing chess.

God, restore to me every contentment
that is possible for a creature
with numbered days.
Stir up desires that make me
reach for more
of what brings life.

I did not invent hope, Lord.
You gave it to me.
Now teach me what to hope for.

reflection prompt

*Our hunger is a powerful indicator of our ability
to hope. Grounded here as we are, what hopes
are rising, even now?*

the pain is too much

My flesh and my heart may fail, but God is the strength of my heart and my portion forever.

—PSALM 73:26 (NRSVUE)

There's a gorgeous Renaissance painting about Icarus, that mythic Greek hero who flew so close to the sun that his waxen wings melted and he fell into the sea and died. In the painting— a rich oil on canvas—we see only a splash and some flailing limbs where Icarus has gone, headfirst, into the water. But the rest of the scene is utterly tranquil. A shepherd has his back turned and is staring placidly at the sky while sheep graze around him. A ship has left port and is sailing away from the drowning man. The poet W. H. Auden captures the tragedy of this image in his poem "Musée des Beaux Arts":

> About suffering they were never wrong,
>
> The Old Masters: how well they understood
>
> Its human position; how it takes place
>
> While someone else is eating or opening a window or just walking dully along.

That is the way of suffering. We are drowning and someone else is looking into the sky. We are terrified and any help is sailing away in the opposite direction. Here is a blessing for that feeling of despair when we feel like we have gone in headfirst. May we feel pulled immediately to shore.

This pain will carry me away.

I am dragging air into my lungs
and watching myself breathe.

I am here, seeing myself from above.
Look how the despair pulls me
toward the rocks.
Watch me row without oars.

Isn't it strange how you know, all at once,
that you can't do this much longer?
But, Lord, this is the great deception:
only this endures.
I am certain about this pain
the way I am sure of nothing else.
I will drown.

But, Jesus, you reach for me.
You steady me.
You repeat my name again and again.
You anchor this boat even as you
slow the current.
You would never leave me like this.

I am busy telling you
I will never survive this
and you tell me the truth.
You never poison me with the lie that
"God gives you what you can handle."
You say, instead,
that you promise,
you swear,
an oath made in your blood,
that this suffering will never outlast
this love.

Tell me again, God,
about how love goes on forever.

No, truly, tell me again
about love stronger than even this.

---

reflection prompt

If you feel any rising despair, repeat to yourself that love is stronger, love is stronger, love is stronger than any undoing. If you're feeling any sense of despair, consider writing it on a sticky note and putting it on the mirror. Pain makes us forget that we are never alone.

for learning to rest

So God blessed the seventh day and hallowed it, because on it God rested from all the work that he had done in creation.

—GENESIS 2:3 (NRSVUE)

We are not exactly a Sabbath culture. We are a RUN AROUND IN EVERY DIRECTION kind of people. And most of our running around, in retrospect, is not for ourselves. Diaper pickup. Doctor's appointment. Did anyone remember milk? When we can't set our work aside, we become like paper thinning to the touch. Here is a blessing for allowing rest to fill up your soul and calm your frayed nerves. You don't just deserve it. You need it.

It's not like I didn't know.

My body knows it too.

Rest.

You promised us rest.

Rest beyond relaxation, recreation,

or the sleep of exhaustion.

Rest that is grounded in the knowledge

that we were never designed to carry it all.

Never meant to be the command center

of the cosmos.

Never meant to solve everything,

fix everything,

nor even be left to our own devices

one whole day.

No. As we stop, we feel our own beginning.

That little sigh.

We are made to rest.

Lord, put your hand in mine.

Lead me to that moment of pause

like we are settling into a park bench.

There.

Here we are.

You created this unfinished world

with my unfinishedness in mind.

Write all my errands in the dirt

beside my feet

and let the wind chase them away.

Here we are in another limited day,

hemmed in by the inevitable panic

of minutes and hours.

So let's pause, shall we?

What a thing you've done.

Bringing me here to steal

moments together.

reflection prompt

It is hard to steal time when we need it the most. Our schedules promise completion if we keep pedaling hard, but they never quite deliver. What is one carefree moment you can give yourself today? A longer shower? Joking around with the next person you meet? God loves our carefree selves, noodling around, doing not much at all.

34

for more love in your life

**But I have calmed and quieted myself, I am like a weaned child with its mother;
like a weaned child
I am content.**

—PSALM 131:2 (NIV)

Envy is so useless. It wearies us. It distracts us. It is the archenemy of gratitude. But isn't envy *so very understandable sometimes*? Other people have the relationships we want, the health we want, the work we want. Other people have the looks and the charisma and the better hair. Wasn't your friend recently on an incredible trip and you were stuck at home with your miserable problems?

Few of us are willing to admit to being jealous. We hide our envy, our achiness, our need for more. But noticing our resentment can also be a good sign. We might be ready to look at it again as a study in light and shadows. Our envy is an expression of our need, and we are hoping that God can infuse our everyday reality with a little more brilliance. What do you really want? What can God and effort and a little love still make possible? Let's see if our envy can be seen from all angles somehow.

I have been propped up on my toes,
peering over fences
but mostly staring at the peeling paint.

Hoping has become longing.
Wanting has become needing.
I can see love everywhere but here.

There is a naturalness to the way
other people experience their joys
popping up like tender, spring grasses.
The earth, it seems, is always warm
and autumn seedlings break open
and bring life, life, everywhere.
And I chew on my lip
as neighbors roll their eyes at
relationships, children, plans—gifts
I would tear open like a Christmas present.

What riches.

Scatter my heart like a dandelion,
drifting high over these walls
and setting down, gently,
where good things grow.
Contentment and wonder,
surprise and new adventure,
comfort in the hands of those
who know love's value and love's cost.
Envy will be blown away by another breeze
and I rest here waiting,
waiting for the blooms.

reflection prompt

*Is a comparison with someone else driving you
a little bananas? Feel so very free to
acknowledge your envy as a good sign that you
are ready for more beauty in your life.*

for breakup, divorce, or heartbreak

He heals the brokenhearted and binds up their wounds.

—PSALM 147:3 (NIV)

Heartbreak is a kind of grief. It is a terrible ending. And yet we are lacking the permission to say that it feels like a death without a funeral. Everyone goes on living and, oh, look, you can find them on social media. Wait, is it just me or do they seem *happier*?

It's complicated. And lonely. And shockingly ongoing because our online and in-person relationships continue to provide evidence that they go on thriving without us. We might worry in moments of brokenness that there isn't spiritual language for how bad it feels. (We think, *Oh, surely people of faith shouldn't be mired in heartbreak or divorce or relationship sadness . . .*) Let's shake off that reluctance and remember that our suffering is a time when God is especially good at being known.

We need God to meet us here in this strange, embarrassing, and awful place. We need God, as the psalmist says, to bind up our wounds. To heal and strengthen us and walk with us as we begin this reinvention. We need God to make something out of the bits and pieces of what is left and surprise us by something, anything, everything new again.

We made plans, Lord.
We strung our hopes together
like glass beads on a cord.

I poured myself into the shape
of that love, Lord,
and it changed me.
Without them, I might have been . . .
who knows?
Someone more.
Someone less.

Friends (bless them) will say:
"GOOD FOR YOU. You are better off."
And I will nod,
except at the bit I can't admit:
I miss the terrible familiarity of who I was.
Who we were.
Who we imagined ourselves to be.

When I step back, I can see how,
in this relationship,
some of my best qualities
grew bright and strong.
I could be courageous and kind,
forgiving and openhearted.

But standing before you, Lord,
I can see how my body curls around

the wounds they left behind:
bitterness and embarrassment,
worry streaked with despair.

I miss them.
I ache to feel the familiarity of their love.
I am tripping over every mention
of the future alone.

Today feels like a funeral without a body.
Walk me through the motions, God—
grief and fear and love—
until I can leave the worst behind.
Love me into a wholeness
I couldn't possibly imagine
here, now,
in the shadow of their love.

---

reflection prompt

What kind of permission do you feel when you treat heartbreak like grief? I find great comfort in small rituals. What if you wore black for a little? What if you felt comfortable bringing them up ALL THE TIME to a good friend and giving yourself an opportunity to grieve pain more openly? Suffering always feels a touch ridiculous but, trust me, it's better to air it out than box it up.

when you're holding on to bad habits

**I do not understand
my own actions.
For I do not do what
I want, but I do the
very thing I hate.**

—ROMANS 7:15 (NRSVUE)

I am researching a book on the history of self-help, so believe me when I say that (a) I have read hundreds of books on habit formation, and (b) there is a reason there are hundreds of books on habit formation. Habits are incredibly difficult to make or break. We know this already because we rarely surprise ourselves. When was the last time you said: "Wow! I had no idea I loved bare-knuckle boxing!" Or "I thought I loved cheesecake but it turns out I only adore pork. Pork for me until the end of time!" We seldom change our preferences. And so too we seldom change our vices.

But when we feel that small tug on our conscience, it is a reminder. We are consistently being poked and prodded by the Holy Spirit (God's sometimes quieter, sometimes louder counterpart). We are meant to change. We are meant to grow into someone more fully able to live in faith, hope, and love. So here is a blessing for letting go of some of the bad habits that prevent us from growing. It's terrible work but it's also sort of wonderful.

Every familiar darkness is dear to me.
My bitterness and gossip.
My condescension and temper.
I cherish my addictions as friends.

Lord, I do not want the searing light
of your truth-telling.
No thanks.
I barely want you to strike a match.

But this is the way of salvation.

You separated good from evil
to hem in our nights.
So I suppose I should let you.

This is the day that the Lord has made.

Lord, pull back the shadows of my heart.
Expose my great comfort
with my favorite sins.

Sustain my hope in your transforming love
as you convince me—
please convince me—
that you are dead-certain,
rising-from-the-dead-certain,
that I'm capable of allowing you
to save me from myself.

reflection prompt

I tend to be very reluctant to confess the sins I know about because I don't want to change them. Truly. I do not want to. Otherwise I would have done it already. What if you admitted a little more by just saying: "God, I wish I wanted to change . . ." And trust that the Holy Spirit can do a lot with a little action like that.

37

make me a peacekeeper

For the Lord your God is God of gods and Lord of lords, the great God, mighty and awesome, who shows no partiality and accepts no bribes. He defends the cause of the fatherless and the widow, and loves the foreigner residing among you, giving them food and clothing. And you are to love those who are foreigners, for you yourselves were foreigners in Egypt.

—DEUTERONOMY 10:17-19 (NIV)

Wherever we stand—however calm it seems at the moment—we are surrounded by spoken or unspoken violence. There are systems that are breaking or broken. There are people whose movements and rights and freedoms are being curtailed. There are laws that soften around money and power, only to harden and punish the poor and weak. As people of faith, we are asked to see the world through their eyes.

Look at the list of those God singles out for justice in the book of Deuteronomy. Our God is the one who accepts no side deals, no tax havens, no lobbyists, no special exceptions. Our God is the one who shelters the weak and demands that injustice be no more. These are the ideals that God sets before us and refuses to answer the question "Isn't that a little idealistic?"

Aren't we being a little too idealistic? Yes, we will answer. After all, God is not on *our* side. We are on *God's* side.

You sent the Holy Spirit.
You sent a dove.
You commanded swords be beaten
into everyday tools.

You sent a baby.
You sent fishermen.
You sent a son to lay his own body down.

We are fools, holy fools.
There must be some
who see lions sheathing
their moistened teeth
and shepherds sent out for lonely lambs.
We cry out, "Save us!" to a God who listens.
Who swears that mass shootings and
missile testing will halt
when the trumpets sound.

Someday you will bend all evil toward love
and melt every bullet into cogs
that turn the wheels of justice.

But until then, Lord, put my body
between the children,
between the imprisoned,
between the widowed,
between the innocents (or not)
and their oppressors,
you made us swear we'd shield
before your kingdom comes.

reflection prompt

Where is the injustice that is near to hand? Is
there a cause that stirs up extra compassion in
your heart? Google around to see if there is a
petition or call to action or community event
sometime soon that you might be willing to join
in some way.

your best life now

For the Lord does not see as mortals see; they look on the outward appearance, but the Lord looks on the heart.

—1 SAMUEL 16:7B (NRSVUE)

The phrase *best life now* was coined in 2004 by a televangelist and, almost overnight, began to dominate popular discourse. In centuries come and gone we might have debated, theologically and philosophically, what constitutes the "good life." Now, the *best life* was the only one worth having.

We are inundated with self-help gospels convincing us that we need to be mastering our lives at all times. It is deeply untrue and, if we are being honest, not a Christian argument. But nonetheless, we feel the pressure to live that way all the time. The writer Anne Lamott has wonderfully sharp things to say about this burden: "Perfectionism is the voice of the oppressor, the enemy of the people. It will keep you cramped and insane your whole life." Amen.

May we be freed from the constant sense that we are supposed to be a breathing show-and-tell of a long list of accomplishments. Hear me now when I say (in my least sanctimonious voice) that only Jesus is perfect. So none of your imperfections are a surprise to God.

My world is spinning on the axis
of a single thought:
I should be living my best life now.

Lord, other people are living their
effortless, joyful, perfect lives.
Why aren't I?
When I scroll social media,
I see grinning faces teaching me, selling me,
convincing me down to every atom
of my not sufficiently moisturized skin
that I should be more.

I could heal myself, budget myself,
shop myself whole.
I am a project ready to be completed.
I am an unfinished checklist.

But that much *is* true.
I am incomplete.
And you never promised us a finished life.

So pry my eyes from the
Christmas card versions
of other people's lives.

God, give me satisfaction in the trying.
Give me joy in the never-quite-there.
Grant me peace in my unsettled heart
for my wild mediocrity.
Help me smile back
at the truth that no one,
not one, knows perfection but you.
And you already looked at this
messy creation
at the beginning of time
and pronounced it pretty darn good.

reflection prompt

*Isn't truth just the best? It brings peace and
calm, and all available joy and satisfaction in
the midst of the unattainable. May you declare
your messiest self to be deeply loved today.*

for a cluttered mind

**Out of my distress I
called on the Lord; the
Lord answered me
and set me free.**

—PSALM 118:5 (ESV)

Some days are like magnets. They accumulate clutter, despite our best efforts. We try to move through the day, but now we're tripping over all that is still unsolved, unfinished, unfinishable. And all our trying just seems to leave new errands behind as reminders of what's left to do, and so our minds too become cluttered spaces.

Where are the clarity and the freedom necessary to be able to do what is important? The "first things" of the kingdom of God. They're under here, somewhere.

The familiar things I touch,
my home, where even in the dark
every corner is known,
the hidden messes, the signs of wear,
the tasks still undone I probably
won't get to,
again.

God, my brain is a junk drawer
stuffed with every worry.
Everything's in there:
the people I'm really worried about,
the world's disasters that seem
to keep getting worse,
the pile of tasks that are as yet undone,
leftovers from yesterday's big projects,
the half-assembled necessities
for tomorrow.
But nothing seems useful.
Nothing will be essential for the
needs of today.

God, I need to get my head on straight.
Have I woken up in the wrong movie?
Maybe the script I'm in is way simpler
than I thought.
Oh, I see! The hero awakes, eats breakfast,
and turns to the one thing necessary—
the pause that connects her to her creator
and the purpose for which she was made.
For love. Nothing else.

Let's shut the drawer.

---

reflection prompt

Dealing with worries can be like playing Whac-A-Mole. They pop up one by one and demand action. Let's decide for a moment that instead of really getting in there (BAM! BAM! BAM! BAM!) we will put down the mallet. I know we can do it. Short breath in . . . long breath out. Again. Again. Again.

being so close to pain, too close

Praise be to the . . . God of all comfort, who comforts us in all our troubles, so that we can comfort those in any trouble with the comfort we ourselves receive from God.

—2 CORINTHIANS 1:3-4 (NIV)

If you are forever close to someone else's pain (or your own), first of all, I'm so sorry. You have suffered, and the aftermath of all suffering is a particular kind of grief and loneliness. When we draw near to pain (or pain draws near to us), we might begin to feel like we are losing any other way of being. Our personalities become less obvious to us. Our normal ways of operating seem strangely distant. Remember small talk? Barely. Remember feeling relaxed when someone said, "How are things?"

We are changed by the suffering we have known. But that doesn't mean that we have to be permanently altered for the worse. Yes, dear heart, you are different. Perhaps, though, we can practice looking at our transformation with so much compassion as we say, *God, I still want every possible good thing. Even now. Especially now.*

Blessed are you who find yourself
near to trauma,
perhaps even the one closest
to the one who has suffered so much.

For you too nothing is the same anymore.

The air has changed
the furniture of your life rearranged
and the cables that once anchored you
to what you knew
have come undone.

Yes, you are doing all you can,
embracing the gift of offering comfort.
Yes, you are doing all the things
you know to do
as the aftermath unfolds.

But, dear one,
let me gently take you aside to say,
this trauma has happened to you too
though you may not feel free to say it.

You too have pain
that may feel too raw and too deep
to excavate and examine just now.
There is so much else to do.

Yet it is there,
telling you in many ways
it will need attention too.
Perhaps even now.

Blessed are you,
gently beginning to name
your own felt needs
and look to the comforts
that will sustain you.

Blessed are you who have discovered
that in your humanity
you have been welcomed into the
community of the wounded.

May you feel all of your own woundedness,
and the tenderness of your own heart,
seen, loved, and held.

reflection prompt

What is the most comforting thing that you do for yourself? I have an overly elaborate face-washing bedtime routine that started when I was sick. I took a minute to say, "Oh, hey, the day was costly but here I am." Do you have a little habit that restores your soul? If you don't, see if you can invent one. (Beverages. Sitting in a certain place. Anything with water. Something can always do the trick.)

when you're awake in the night

Peace I leave with you; my peace I give you.

—JOHN 14:27A (NIV)

If you see columnist David Brooks around somewhere, please let him know that I have spent the last few nights in a semisleep fugue state thinking about an article he wrote. And then combining his argument with an apocalyptic vision of zombies taking over an airport while I am waiting for a flight. It was terrifying and absurd, and utterly normal for me. I waste my sleeping hours with an exciting combination of self-sabotage, annoyance, embarrassment, and fear. Isn't the untethered mind wonderful?

Most of the loveliest ancient prayers for such occasions center on the image of the watchtower. A watchtower is a high place from which a guard can see for miles while everyone else can, as the saying goes, "let down their guard." An ancient prayer from Augustine asks God to "keep watch . . . with those who work, or watch, or weep this night." Beautiful. These invocations say, again and again, some version of *God, will you be appropriately alert because I am supposed to be unconscious.* This is exactly what we need God to do. We have come to the limits of our vigilance, our abilities, our emotional self-management, and our physical energy. Now, God, please keep watch over our humanity.

Oh, God, I long for sleep,
and the natural restoration it brings,
for body, mind, and soul.

But here I am, feeling ridiculous.
Aren't other people supposed to be
asleep at this hour,
not scrambling for solutions?

But this is another kind of normal,
the regular interruption that I keep
thinking won't happen again,
but it does, and it has. Again.

So I do all the things I know to do.
Yet here I am, still awake.

God, this is endless.
And I know I won't be functional.
Let's do something about this.
Tomorrow, after a nap.
Let's leave the problem-solving until then.
Right now, return me to myself.

Let me be legs that sink heavily
into this mattress,
and arms that fall loosely by my sides.

Let me be eyes that stop itching
for my phone
and are (soon to be) heavy and closed.

Let my heart slow into that soft
and even beat
that says, there is nothing, nothing,
nothing to do
but be.

reflection prompt
*Take out a notepad and put it beside your bed.
(Don't use your phone. Your phone is a tar pit of
entertainment.) When you wake up, or can't
sleep, scribble down any to-dos or especially
buzzy thoughts. No judgment. Can you imagine
leaving those worries on the table for another
day?*

when anxiety rises

Do not be anxious about anything, but in every situation, by prayer and petition, with thanksgiving, present your requests to God.

—PHILIPPIANS 4:6 (NIV)

I hold my thoughts on a leash, dragging them around. Didn't I do something really stupid this morning? Probably. What did I say again? Oh, let me pull that around too. I revise and revise, stew and replay. I am fairly certain that somewhere out there people are probably pretty annoyed at me, at the very least.

Does your mind churn too? What category of thoughts take up too much space? Family, work, dating, love, kids? Or are your worries more diffuse, fogging up a clear mind for no particular reason? When I am trying to release these worries to God, I imagine that, instead of a leash, I am holding a series of helium balloons. Each carrying its own weight. And, oh look, I just let go. Now they can float around the ceiling at will. If I need one later, I can fish for it, but, truly, who needs another worry?

Let's bless our anxious hearts with a peace that God is particularly good at giving.

God, it doesn't seem possible
to align my anxious self to your word
that says to me:
"Don't be anxious about anything."
Because I'm already stewing.
I'm a worrier, and you already know that.
So here we are.
And here I am, being what I am.

God, open your heart to mine
and pour in your peace.
Let your mind flow into these
scattered thoughts
that seem to want to cling to worries
And coalesce like metal filings to a magnet.
I need your spirit to bless me
with a calm that isn't mine to create.

Bless all my stubbornness and
allow me to, wonderfully,
just give up for a moment.
To stop fighting my own needs
and concerns.

And if I can barely do it,
bless even the trying to try
(for that's roughly all I'm able to do,
and I smile to think that even this
pleases you).

Bless my will to will that anxiety
be lifted away,
that when worries arise,
I can say to them, "Go on,
keep rising all the way to God
who can handle this."
I'll pray them up, up, up, and away.

reflection prompt

*Sit somewhere comfortable and let your body
soften. Let the air comfortably expand the
spaces that are easily fillable. Breathe out and
mix the air with the thought that worries you,
giving it to God to take for a minute. Let
yourself pause and rest, with nothing to do.
And in your own time, continue until you feel
yourself sighhhhh. You'll hear it. That's when
you're done, love.*

honest faith

Trust in the Lord with all your heart and lean not on your own understanding.

—PROVERBS 3:5 (NIV)

Nowadays, with the triumph of gentle, therapeutic ways of speaking about prayer, we might entirely forget that our blessings and prayers can be completely offensive in the best way. I have a colleague here at my university with a reputation for being joyfully outrageous, and he makes me laugh so hard because I honestly cannot believe what he can get away with. His name is Stanley Hauerwas and, for instance, when he was asked to pray a nice, vague, feel-good prayer at a serious university luncheon to people in suits and ties, he prayed something like this instead: "God . . . we do not fear you, since we prefer to fear one another. . . . You have, of course, tried to scare the hell out of some of us through the creation of your people Israel and through the life, death, and resurrection of Jesus. But we are subtle, crafty, and stiff-necked people who prefer to be damned into vagueness." Oh, I read the transcript of this later and *wept*. Hysterical. And, word has it, Stanley ruined public prayer for everyone else. Now the university holds a moment of silence instead.

That's always the trickiest part of speaking spiritually: when do we call people out? And when do we change people with grace? Here's a blessing for the need for that kind of honest faith and the right amount of love to accompany it.

God, I am disappointed and embarrassed
at what people get up to
in the name of religion.

My heart is thirsty for a faith I can trust.
And I mean that.
I don't trust the cultural scripts
that turn religion into any game
where somebody wins
and somebody loses,
and there is the strong scent
of the entrepreneur.
Somebody is selling something.

And from the recesses of my mind
from some very early encounter,
I think I must have met the real you, God.
That somehow I met goodness so pure
it settled my heart to understand
trustworthiness of a majesty and stature
that thereafter I could accept
no counterfeits.

God, come and show yourself again.
Show me faith that cannot be faked.

Let me see you in the loveliness of others
living out their faith so genuinely,
so honestly,
that you shine through.

And if I can't get all the theology right,
let me not worry too long.
I suspect you'd rather I live honestly
by the light of what I know to do
that looks most like you,
and keep quiet about the rest.

reflection prompt

*Think of a person you know who is incredibly
gracious about disagreement. What are some
of their methods for cultivating grace?*

for a funeral

For with much wisdom comes much sorrow; the more knowledge, the more grief.

—ECCLESIASTES 1:18 (NIV)

When someone dies, we are thrown into emptiness and unreality. Those we love have grown like vines around our hearts. So when death comes, there is a wrenching, a tearing away at the root. People will try to say comforting things about our loved one's advanced age perhaps, or their having lived long or meaningful lives. Or maybe they can't say much at all because our person died early, suddenly, or with an incompleteness that looms over us.

But the truth is that we are not simply in mourning, we are lovesick. Death is an affront to love itself. I find this to be one of the greatest and worst of all of God's mysteries: how the more we do what God commanded—love and love and love—the worse this pain becomes. The more we love, the more we cannot imagine an end to it. There is a poem by Emily Dickinson that imagines God "in the fair schoolroom of the sky" explaining each separate anguish. But in the meantime, we are here. We are left with the weight of wondering why—why our love feels like a gift and a curse.

You know I don't believe that faith is a solution to the problem of pain. But I do believe that God guarantees us God's actual presence. So let's see where that takes us. And in the meantime, I am so sorry this has happened to you, to them, and to us all.

If there ever was such a thing
as normal life,
it has slowed to a stop now.
Lord, I have loved and lost.
The world is empty.

I am swimming in the unreality of this end,
this impossible ending,
for we are trying to live in both
the before and the after.

Carry me. Carry us.
Carry every stage of this moment
when we can shout and cry,
prepare food and file our paperwork,
and feel weary and sad and joyful
and numbness because
the totality of death will never, ever
feel final.

In our conversations there is a raw feeling
we are holding back,
drawing a gauzy veil over all the unease.
Will people feel honored, valued, needed?
Will there be awkwardness
among friends and family?
God, give us room to breathe and to mourn,
and perhaps even to laugh together.
Help us be our best selves.

Blessed are we, trying to manage
the unmanageable,
the fact that this is a final parting.
No, this is the *second last* parting.
But we will see them again, you promised.
One has gone from us down a path
we cannot see.
And we must stand and mourn,
at a distance.

God, make this a good funeral, somehow.
Let love live here.
Let it fill us, even in our loss,
that we might receive comfort
beyond the measure that we ourselves
can hold,
that there might be some—dear God,
let there be some—to share.

reflection prompt

*Jesus says that blessed are those who mourn,
which is precisely when we feel exiled from any
sense of blessing. But I believe in those words is
a promise: God draws near to the suffering. So
that's it. Nothing to do except say, "God, you
said you would be there. Be here now."*

noticing beauty

Consider the lilies, how they grow: they neither labor nor spin; but I tell you, not even Solomon in all his glory clothed himself like one of these.

—LUKE 12:27 (NASB)

Are you a noticer? Litter on the side of the road. Dust on the windowsill. The placement of napkins on a well-laid table. Some people have an incredible eye for detail. They know where things go and if they should be there at all. I have a noticing mother-in-law who *delights* in highway landscaping. She will see pansies or a cluster of tall bushes and audibly gasp. She has found the ability to experience the world as a sensory buffet.

I, on the other hand, would probably have to be struck by lightning to notice these things. In fact, I worked in a restaurant that was struck by lightning and burned to the ground twice, so you'd think I would be more observant. But I have to remind myself not simply to look, but to *behold.* So let's bless the gift of cultivated attention. May it bring us endless *ooooh*s and *aahhhhh*s.

It's not every day that you see it,
but sometimes beauty sneaks up on you
with a tenderness, a sweetness, so lovely
it hurts.

It sings to the heart
and makes it glad
that ever a baby laughed
or a parent smiled
at the hilarious solemnity of play.

Beauty brings a kind of grief.
Because its perfection rings so true

it calls out everything else
that has ever fallen short.
In me. In us. In everything.

But that's the thing.
It's just the way of it:
that beauty will always be
crushingly lovely.
We are grass. We are fireflies.
We are the day that the Lord has made.

reflection prompt

Today or tomorrow I want you to go find
something you are delighted by: birds,
macaroni and cheese, whatever. It's out there
somewhere.

Have a Beautiful, Terrible Lent!

What Is Lent?

Lent marks the forty days leading up to Jesus's murder and surprising return to life three days later. It is a practice that began during the fourth century as a way to prepare Christians for the holiest, hardest days of our story.

During Lent, we ask God to show us the world as it is. We begin with the reality of our finitude rubbed on our foreheads on Ash Wednesday—from dust we were made, to dust we shall return. Then, we walk through that reality in a kind of dress rehearsal. It's the downward slope of God—the Great Descent. The whole church must descend to the depths with their savior.

Frankly, Lent is my favorite part of the church calendar. Suddenly, all of us are on the losing team. And we look at each other with well-earned wonder, horror, and awe. We begin to tell each other the truth again: life is so beautiful and life is so hard. For everyone.

Of course, the cross isn't the end of the story. But this season of grief is carved out to acknowledge the reality of Jesus's sacrifice. Our savior knew pain and grief and despair, and so do we. Easter is coming, yes. But for now, we sit in the ashes of our broken dreams and broken hearts, knowing that God sits here with us.

What am I supposed to do?

Many people practice Lent by giving something up—alcohol, meat, chocolate, social media. Some take up something new—a new prayer practice or swearing profusely, like I did one year. (It's a ridiculous story about how when I thought I was going to die, I had a rather profane response to Lent. You are more than welcome to read about my tirades in my memoir *Everything Happens for a Reason (and Other Lies I've Loved)*). But perhaps your desire to try a new Lenten practice could simply be reading an entry in this book every day.

If you'd like to use this book as your daily practice, lovely! I have put the next forty blessings in an order that you might use in the days leading up to Lent. If you're not sure *when* to begin, you're not alone. The start date changes, so it's very confusing. Just type "Ash Wednesday" into your internet browser and the date you find will be the day to start. Over the next few years, Lent starts on these dates:

2024	February 14		2029	February 14
2025	March 5		2030	March 6
2026	February 18		2031	February 26
2027	February 10		2032	February 11
2028	March 1		2033	March 2

One additional note: You get to take Sundays off. They're little breaks to remind you that you get to rest and celebrate a little even in the midst of suffering. In fact, that's usually when we need it most.

Toward the end of Lent, the experience culminates in what we call "Holy Week." Holy Week is the way we remember the events leading up to Jesus's death (Good Friday) and his coming back from the dead (Easter Sunday). We remember how scared he was. How his friends betrayed and abandoned him. How he loved them anyway. He was put on trial and then publicly humiliated and strung up to die. But then . . . it's an incredibly hard-to-believe story (anyone who says otherwise apparently has seen a lot more people resurrected than I have). But it's the truth on which we hang our own understanding of life and death. We believe that because of Jesus, we don't simply die. We are forgiven and loved and gathered up to be with God and each other forever.

Lent is full of hard truths. And it is a perfect moment for the spiritual honesty we are practicing here. We can look on this tragicomedy with love and bemusement as we wait for the *someday* that will be God's promised future. There, God's kingdom comes. God's will be done on earth as it is in heaven. And in the meantime, there's this . . . our beautiful, terrible days.

for Ash Wednesday

The Lord is compassionate and gracious,
slow to anger, abounding in love.
He will not always accuse,
nor will he harbor his anger forever;
he does not treat us as our sins deserve
or repay us according to our iniquities.
For as high as the heavens are above the earth,
so great is his love for those who fear him;
as far as the east is from the west,
so far has he removed our transgressions from us.
As a father has compassion on his children,
so the Lord has compassion on those who fear him;
for he knows how we are formed,
he remembers that we are dust.

—PSALM 103:8-14 (NIV)

Did you not know
what the Holy One
can do with dust?

—JAN RICHARDSON

Holy day suggestion: If you google around, you can find an Ash Wednesday service or a simple "drop by for ashes" situation. It's so nice. (And it's short! Did I talk you into it yet?) Someone will bless you and smear a cross of ashes on your forehead. No one really expects you to know what you're doing so you don't have to feel self-conscious. But it's deeply moving as someone says, gently and startlingly, "From dust you came and to dust you will return."

These days of dust.

These days of despair.

We can hear reality speak to us

in a clear, ringing voice.

So we approach. Carefully. Barely ready

to hear the hard truths we long to be told

about beautiful, terrible death.

How strange that it feels so right and good

to walk forward together

wearing our finitude,

a mess of ash smeared on our foreheads

to be told:

remember that you are dust,

and to dust you shall return.

How strange that it feels so right and good

at the edge of awareness

—the balance point

of being and nonbeing.

I catch my breath as I turn and look

to see the shining faces all around.

I see it all in a glance:

how precious

how precious

how precious

how holy each single, imperfect life,

how beautiful

how great

how unconquerable

each single, unfinishable life,

because you deemed it so.

You looked on us, covered in death,

as a man about to walk a darkening path,

the only one who could wipe away

our ashes

with a single act of love.

reflection prompt

*If this is your first time doing any Lent-y stuff,
welcome! And if you are already a pro, well
done. Is there a thing you'd like to give up?
Giving something up is how we practice the
feeling of being stripped down. Is there
something you'd like to take on instead? Every
season is different, so choose something that
helps you feel more connected to God's losing
team.*

to feel a little more grateful

But blessed are your eyes because they see, and your ears because they hear.

—MATTHEW 13:16 (NIV)

The moment we want to make any spiritual progress, we immediately feel how difficult it is. Do you want to feel more grateful? Wonderful. Now you feel a lot of pressure to be grateful and you wonder if you ought to be the kind of person who yells "I LOVE THIS" at every red light in traffic. But gratitude is part of our ability to notice. We might notice the big realities of the day: *Thank you for this paycheck! Thank you that this doctor is better than the last one!* Or our gratitude might be incredibly minute and ultimately eclipsed by other feelings: *Well, God, this addiction is so depressing but this hour was okay.* Either way, we are building our capacity to do this hard work. The better we get at gratitude, the better we can get at noticing smaller and smaller reminders of God's goodness. We might notice the softness of someone's hand we get to hold. We might notice how much a television show really makes us laugh. Gratitude is not a solution to suffering, but it sure does make the rest of existence more meaningful.

I piled my small joys in heaps,
like mounds of autumn leaves on a lawn,
but they've blown away.

I have known thankfulness
but it all feels too scattered now.

So let's start again, shall we?

Perhaps I'll begin by . . .
taking off my socks (who can stop me?).
Silencing my phone from its buzzing.
Sighing like I am writing on a clipboard
how deeply disappointed I am.
I am.

All right.

Lord, what shade of blue is that
in the shifting sky?
And why does it settle me
to light a candle?
Let me strike a match for the sheer
pleasure of the sound it makes.
These small hopes pull me on.

Lord, the sound of laughter is there, faintly,
if I strain for it.
And the way kids laugh, God,

it's contagious.
And why hasn't anyone curbed the number
of eyelashes per child?
It's ridiculous. Absolutely useless.
It's a marvel.

Remind me of a love that is good
and let the warmth of it
tug loose a memory
of being seen and loved, even cherished
by a familiar, knowing face.

They're here within reach.
These loves.
The kindling of gratitude when I start
to count and count and count again.

reflection prompt

*Deciding to ask God to help you feel grateful is
a truly radical act. It doesn't negate the truth
of what is deeply sad or disappointing but sets
alongside it that other truth that slipped from
view. The fact that this world is beautiful and
good too. Would you try to practice gratitude
for a moment? Just turn to God and say, "Okay.
Show me something good."*

for living without control

He has shown you, O mortal, what is good. And what does the Lord require of you? To act justly and to love mercy and to walk humbly with your God.

—MICAH 6:8 (NIV)

I had a very tender podcast conversation with theologian and ethicist Stanley Hauerwas. We have worked together for almost two decades now, and I rely on him to be incredibly certain about what makes a life good and virtuous. But he was telling me about how incredibly painful life has been for him. How was his first marriage, to a woman with severe mental illness? Hell, he said. (I love him for many reasons, and his bluntness is one of them.) But after describing how many twists and turns that life had taken, he had come to a conclusion: "The ability to live well is the ability to live without so many certainties."

We will have to develop a high tolerance for having so little control and so few bedrock assumptions. So let's ask our God to "unplan" our days a little and help us live that way.

God, I come to you as I am.
It is all I have, really.
And the next one I'm conscious of
will be the same.
I can feel the way I move,
moment to moment,
without the comfort of "solutions."

It seems wild to me now how I imagined
any once-and-for-all cure for this,
or a master plan to ensure things
will work out.
But, truth be told, that's always been
my secret hope.

So, Lord, let's try again.
I'm begging for a new plan.
I want a plan that is an "unplan."
I must keep moving and planning,
trying and changing,
knitting my days together even as
they unravel.
So can we do this together?

Remind me to pray: come Lord
and quiet the worry.
I step, and you steady me.
I give, and you keep my hands open.
I act, and you fortify me with courage
to try and try and try again.

This life is uncertain, Lord,
but your love is not.
You tell the story of my life
regardless of how little I know
about how it ends, except to say,
you were there since the beginning
and you appear on every page.

reflection prompt

*Now that we know that we don't know, let's
enjoy that thought for a moment. Isn't it
delicious that the God who flung stars into
space also knows every beginning and end? So
let's settle in for a moment and let ourselves
not know in the presence of the God who
already knows.*

for that unsettled feeling

Now there is great gain in godliness with contentment, for we brought nothing into the world, and we cannot take anything out of the world.

—1 TIMOTHY 6:6-7 (ESVUK)

I don't find a lot of natural contentment, do you? At my worst, I stir up my own longings. I feel the ache of my desires because I am acting on less-than-flattering habits of jealousy, ambition, or resentment. Sometimes I lack peace because I have not taken stock of my own actions and exhibit a shocking unwillingness to act to help myself. Or I blame others for not meeting needs I probably didn't express well in the first place. Sound familiar? If not, honestly, good for you. That's wonderful.

Perhaps you are not stirring up any trouble . . . trouble comes to you. You might be feeling unsettled because you are experiencing the cost of what is already good in your life. You are loving and trying and helping, and all of it hurts. As bell hooks wrote, "The practice of love offers no place of safety. We risk loss, hurt, pain. We risk being acted upon by forces outside our control." If that's you, you feel a lack of contentment because there is never enough.

Whether there is enough or there is never enough, perhaps we could pray for some of that ephemeral peace that God promises. We can fill ourselves up with a moment of divine calm. Here we go.

Fulfillment. Contentment. I swear
I've had it for a minute or two.

Every lovely feeling is made of sand today.
Peace slips through my cupped hands.

There's a version I keep hoping for
where every good memory is a brick
stacked up to wall out every pain,
every remorse, every stinging fear.

But it never works that way.
No matter what I do
to build up my reserves
I find myself at the mercy
of every new negative feeling.

Contentedness feels elusive.
Fulfillment feels inaccessible.

But ours is not a story built on emotion.
Sometimes we will feel
the truth of your love,
our purpose, our intense belongingness,
and the rest of the time
we will have to shrug
and wait for any settled feeling to return.

Our feelings come and go
but your stubborn love remains.
Your hope stays.
Your peace, when we reach for it,
will be placed in our hands
like a dove.

Settle me.
Slow my unsteady pulse.
Remind me that, even if I were to have
every "perfect" feeling,
the sheer fact that nothing lasts
is an enormous comfort right now.
This ache will pass.
You're here.
You're here.

reflection prompt

*Put your hand on your heart. Or rest your
hands gently on your lap. Or lie down because,
hey, who else is going to tell you to do that?
Breathe in and out. Imagine peace like a little
bird in front of you. (I once had many, many
birds land on me at once, and let's not imagine
that. It's not peaceful at all. Just pick one bird
who really likes you.) But feel that delicate
sense of peace land, and then settle in with it.*

First Sunday of Lent

Stop. Relax. Celebrate and Rest.

to feel more love

See what kind of love the Father has given to us, that we should be called children of God; and so we are. The reason why the world does not know us is that it did not know him.

—1 JOHN 3:1 (ESV)

The stories we have about ourselves can be so loud. That we are never good enough. Never beautiful enough. Never lovable enough. Never talented enough. The list goes on forever. But then we have a God who looks at us with love that feels implausible. Right? So let's make God's love for us feel a little more bearable, and quiet the terrible voices for the moment.

I am going to put them down:
every insecurity and ugly belief I have
about my body, my abilities,
my personality.

They won't teach me anything.
(At least not now.)

Let me accept your love like a compliment,
Oh thanks.
That's so kind of you.
You shouldn't have.

Let me accept other people's love
like a wrapped present.
For me?
That's so thoughtful.
It's exactly what I wanted.

Lord, I've spent so much time
imagining my worst qualities
that it's difficult to imagine that you
numbered the hairs on my head,
painted my eyes this color,
and soften at the sound of my voice.

You are not the bathroom scale
or a work evaluation.
You are not every ex-partner or ex-friend.
You know the very best of me.
You are my cheerleader and champion,
my memory keeper and favorite friend.
Flood me with love, love, love
because of who I am, who I've become,
and who you made me.

The world is loud, God.
Only you can convince me
of how embarrassingly lovable I can be.
Quiet the shame and doubt
and self-hatred.
I'm ready to feel love again.

---

reflection prompt

The heart-melting love of a parent for a child taking her first steps. The glistening eyes of a friend who hurts when you hurt. All the qualities of the best parent or friend or partner one could imagine, only better. That's the love God has for you. Could you find divine love and other people's love a little more bearable today? Try a simple exercise like accepting the next compliment you receive. Just say: "Thank you. I needed that."

when your family disappoints you

In this world you will have trouble. But take heart!

—JOHN 16:33B (NIV)

"No one loves you like your family." Has anyone said that to you? It's such a common way of describing the most valuable ties that bind us to each other and to our lives. Our families become the centerpiece of every form of belonging, every life lesson, every necessary sacrifice.

But so often our families are also places of deep wounding. They did not love *us* the way we needed. We could not love *them* the way they needed. We become locked inside loops and loops of painful ways of relating to each other. Our families are not always who we hoped they could be, and change seems virtually impossible. So what then? Here's a blessing for some honest grief about the disappointment that comes from the ties that bind.

God, it was a good enough plan, wasn't it?
To gather and just be a family again?

Didn't I take care of all contingencies?
Pour in creativity and generosity?
Hope rose in me like a hot-air balloon
on a summer's day.

Lord, I know you promise an easy yoke
and a lightness of spirit
that surpasses any reasonable measure,
but today I carry this hurt like a stone.

I need the love we genuinely have
for each other
to carry some of this weight,
to carry us through these hours together.

God, what will it take?
Why is healing so long in coming?
Oh my soul, what am I to do with this
sadness?

I release it into your hands.

I fly like a bird to your rest
and make my home in you.
Make me feel settled in love.
Make me wise in discernment.
Help me see clearly, love generously,
and protect my tender, worried heart.
In you lies every good beginning
and every beautiful, possible ending.

reflection prompt

*Think about a role you play in your family
system. Perhaps you are the helpful one or the
"check out and just survive" one. Maybe you
are the discouraged one or the incredibly
cheerful one. All right. Now think of the person
in your life who really knows you best. Are you
different when you are with that person? What
can we learn about who God wants us to
become when we picture ourselves with people
who love us best?*

finding God's presence

Where can I go from your Spirit? Where can I flee from your presence? If I go up to the heavens, you are there; if I make my bed in the depths, you are there. If I rise on the wings of the dawn, if I settle on the far side of the sea, even there your hand will guide me, your right hand will hold me fast.

—PSALM 139:7-10 (NIV)

Once or twice the presence of God has fallen on me like an anvil. And I thought, *Oh boy, I hope I don't have anything to do for the rest of my life except love God.* (Turns out that loving God is very time consuming.) But those moments of divine interruption are probably rare. God's nearness will probably pop up in our lives as an act of cultivated attention. It's a little like Oh look! There's God. How odd that this is precisely the moment when I set aside a few minutes to notice God's presence at all.

It's good news and bad news, of course. Good news: God wants to be found by us. Bad news: We might need to go looking. Here's a blessing for the moments when we might need a push.

God of all that we hardly notice,
ruler of the ground under our feet
and the sky stretched over our heads.

Send your spirit to direct our steps
and our thoughts
as we stumble around this day and night.

We have too much to do, so give us
enough silence to hear your voice.
We have too much to worry about,
so quiet us with a moment of your peace.
We have too much to carry,
so lighten our hearts with your love.

We are your people, eyes cast
down on the ground that you made,
wary that the sky will fall again.
Remind us again that above and below

you are here.

---

reflection prompt

*I love this prayer by the monk Thomas Merton:
"The fact that I think I am following your will
does not mean that I am actually doing so. But
I believe that the desire to please you does in
fact please you." Can that be our prayer today?
We can try to try to want to try.*

to keep moving

**Wait for the Lord. Be
strong and take heart,
and wait for the Lord!**

—PSALM 27:14 (EHV)

As Christians, we are asking to keep going, keep walking, keep
hoping. Our language of faith and hope, specifically, is predicated
on our belief that God is asking us to keep moving. But that
requires a certain kind of bravery . . . the kind that moves into
uncertainty with determination.

I asked *New York Times* columnist Frank Bruni on the *Everything
Happens* podcast about moving forward, since he thinks a lot
about it. After a stroke in his eye left him with significant vision
loss, Frank had to entirely reinvent not only how he worked but
how he could tolerate a future with long stretches of darkness,
literal and emotional. How did he do it? He said that he became a
student of his friends. What are they dealing with? It's not always
visible to the naked eye. "If you do that," he concluded, "you
quickly have a different context and realize that the bad fortune
that you have been dealt is much more universal than it is
exceptional." His admiration for the people around him gave him
endless small lessons in managing the endless unknowns of this
life.

We are asking to wake up every morning and keep moving. But
uncertainty can be terrifying. Let's try to bless the unknownness
of this day.

Lord, the big arc of your salvation story
is spread across eternity.
You made us and we fall,
you save us and we rise,
hand clutching hand,
until our stories all become one
with yours forever.

But today, I wait.
I wait for the flicker in the darkness,
the candle in the window,
the next sign to direct me
as I lurch forward
in all-encompassing dark.

I may as well be doing this
with my eyes closed.

But that's faith, isn't it?
Lord, how even now,
with my eyelids squeezed shut,
I can see the sweep of your story,
us falling and rising,
you reaching to steady us,
pulling us ever forward to you,
through this soon-to-be-fading dark.

reflection prompt
*Could we try that? Make a study of our friends.
Who keeps going? Who is teaching us about
living with the unknown?*

for deep tiredness

**Hear my cry, O God; listen to my prayer.
From the ends of the earth I call to you,
I call as my heart grows faint.**

—PSALM 61:1–2A (NIV)

Strangely, it's when we are most tired that it is hardest to seek rest. We put off the idea of a break as we buzz and hum with an energy that is beyond our natural capacity. There's always one more thing to do. *Isn't there a load of laundry? Shoot, I should call and check in on so-and-so.* And the more we press on, the more it seems like proof that we don't need to accept our limitations at all.

But that's just putting our sad and gloopy brains in charge. (Yes, *gloopy* is now our favorite word.) We do not need to be propelled by a fight-or-flight existence. Or if we are, we must imagine it as a season and continue to ask for more and more help as we get our bearings. Because you, my dear, are not bionic. So let's bless all those tired bones.

God of shelter,

clear a place of sacred rest,

for my strength is failing.

Shelter me from every fear,

real or imagined.

Slow my hummingbird heart.

Steer each coming storm

away from this quiet place

where, tucked into your arms,

I am hidden in your love.

reflection prompt

Let's find a blanket and sigh in God's direction. I swear that "deep fatigue and/or sorrow" summarizes half of the Psalms, so feel free to consider it spiritual.

God, lead me

**Whoever follows me will
never walk in darkness,
but will have the light
of life.**

—JOHN 8:12B (NIV)

Over and over Jesus says, "Follow me." But I'm not a natural
follower. In fact, I would like there to be a separate moving
walkway in the airport for people like me, who lose their ever-living
minds if they have to break their gait while power walking. I would
prefer that God catch me while I'm in a dead sprint, now that we're
talking about it.

Other times I am hardly going anywhere at all. Some manner of
undoing has dismantled all my plans and the only word I would use
to describe myself is *stuck*. God, how can I follow you if I never
seem to be going anywhere?

Here's a little blessing for the moments of too-fast and the
moments of too-slow. May we learn what it means to follow
somehow.

God, go and I will follow.

Because, truly, I cannot lead.

I cannot drag myself forward,
chin up and eyes on the horizon,
when all I see is the mud
caking around my feet.

God, go and grace will follow.
I've seen it all before.
How in the smallest moments,
the tiniest efforts
multiply in your wake.

We've seen the sun rise
over an empty tomb
and life spring up from nothing but dust,
so, all things considered,
I suppose I should finally believe
that you could do a lot with this day,
my life, and these weary limbs,
and learn to follow
the God who goes first.

reflection prompt

*Are you the very speedy type? A little sluggish?
Or are you dragged down by life? What does
"following God" mean to you in this season of
life?*

Second Sunday of Lent

You get a break.

love, love, love

Love one another deeply, from the heart.

—1 PETER 1:22B (NIV)

Love, love, love—the simplest word and the most complicated act. Our love sucks us into errands. Our love bends our dreams toward other people's fulfillment. Our love is often directly at odds with our ability to rest, play, eat, sleep, or even have much time for the people we love. (*Can I get an AMEN?*)

It's the strangest phenomenon and one we all understand because we have seen it up close. The more we love ... then the more we love. There is no scarcity in love. There is a scarcity of time and resources, yes, but love grows and grows. I was trying to explain this to my son, who was exhibiting characteristically *zero* subtlety in asking who I love more. Do I love the next-door neighbor more? Do I love other children more? If I had more children would they go to the top of the list?

"Oh, hon, it's the weirdest thing. But when you love people, it's like they move into your house. But your home mysteriously multiplies and makes more rooms to put everybody," I said, finally.

"Where am I then?" he asked.

"The living room," I replied.

"Great," he said definitively. "I guess Dad can have the garage."

Ahhhh, the generosity of the human heart. But I stand by my argument. Where love is concerned, it's an Open House.

Lord, the shadowed world
is full of troubles.
So give me the good,
inconvenient work of love.

Link my life to others
so that their worries
become my own.
Give me errands I don't want
which ease the burdens of others.
Divert me from the plans I've made
to zip from A to B
when you have better ideas.
Put my hands to work
with a less-grumbling heart
and let their dreams drift into my own.

You've given me tools to use
and ideas to fashion
that will bring me neither recognition,
nor money, nor praise.

You've made love such a sneaky thing.
The more we love as you do,
the less we are keeping track of it at all.

reflection prompt

Humor me on this one: in your life-house, who lives there? Who was the last person to move in? Let's thank God for them.

waiting for anything good to happen

**With all my heart,
I am waiting, Lord, for you!
I trust your promises.**

—PSALM 130:5 (CEV)

Our Christian story has a lot in it about waiting. God makes the world in stages. Jesus dies and then we wait for his resurrection. And then when he is raised from the dead and goes to heaven, he really takes his sweet time coming back to earth again. Waiting is why we need hope. But I find waiting to be incredibly difficult. Maybe you do too, so let's see if we can bless us impatient types.

You who wait
under a starless sky
worried about eternity.
Eternity *without*.
An absence that threatens to
hollow out the earth.

You who wait
in your own heart's cavernous room
bouncing worries off the walls.
Hello?
Is anyone there?
How long, how long, how long?

While you wait
let us imagine the sky sinking lower, lower,
close enough to see a winking star or two.

While you wait
let us imagine this room's walls
shrinking, narrowing,
closing to the size
of a comfortable living room.

Ahhhh.
There we are.

Lord, in the endlessness of these aches,
my soul's unanswered calls,
my own unfinished incompleteness,
close me in.
Close me in
to a space small enough
to enclose this tender heart of mine
and soften every worry about forever
except the ongoingness of this love.

reflection prompt
*Everything shrinks down to this: Love has
come. What can you do to downsize your life to
love today?*

seeing God everywhere

Now faith is the assurance of things hoped for, the conviction of things not seen.

—HEBREWS 11:1 (NRSVUE)

A few years ago I was asked to write a piece for *The New York Times* about the nature of hope. And I mention that esteemed paper because I was more than flattered . . . I was propelled into wanton acts of boasting. I told everyone in my family and then all of my friends. I would be part of a great act of public optimism. Whatever I wrote would be featured in a roundup of other news items that were ostensibly similar and it would be featured on New Year's Day so we could all be very, very hopeful together.

So I asked, what else is there to be hopeful about? What would the other pieces talk about? 1. Bees. 2. Soccer.

3. An extremely mild curtailment of human rights violations against women in India but it's not looking promising for the future. But maybe the bees are coming back? I asked. Probably not, replied my editor.

And that is how it seems most days—that even when we want to be profoundly hopeful, we end up taking most of it back. So here's to the moments of believing that there is more hope than we can see.

This world feels solid,
through and through.
Nothing is more obvious than
who's in and who's out—
the numbers at the bottoms of these
credit card bills,
and the worry lines
around our eyes and mouths.

Just ask anyone.
Nothing is happening except headlines
and a new season on Netflix
and the rumbling of wars, near and far.

Then we squint.

There you are. Shimmering at the edges
of some extravagant act of love.

There you are. Quickening our steps
toward your surprising favorites:

the weak and poor and scared,
the lasts-becoming-firsts,
those who can't squeeze
through the eye of the needle.

There you are. Calling us strong
when we are weak.
Telling us to link arms
with those who suffer.
Explaining how justice
will invert the order of things.

The world feels solid,
through and through, God.
Help me squint and see you better.

---

reflection prompt

Squinting is recalibration. It's a partial shutting out in order to see better. It blurs what is clearly superfluous or downright distracting so light can infuse even that. What would you see today if you squinted a little? (Other than that you might need reading glasses, which are now available affordably in many colors and styles online. Let me know if that works too.)

well, I'm not all that great sometimes

Teach me your way, O Lord, that I may walk in your truth.

—PSALM 86:11A (NRSVUE)

We are great mysteries to ourselves. And never is that more true than when we are doing something terrible. Who, me? I have no idea how I made that mistake. Again. And again. Cut to me opening a letter outlining my sins and scribbling this reply: "Dear Sir or Madam, Even though it is *entirely in my wheelhouse* to do exactly the bad thing you are describing, I am shocked to receive word of this recent news. Sincerely yours, Me."

My faults are typically things I cherish, like gifts I give myself. Too much anger. Too much pride. Too much unforgiveness. I look in the direction of transformation and declare it impossible, so I return home with the sins I brought with me. If you need a little gentle language for your own confession, you might try this blessing. Demystifying our own faults is difficult without believing that we are loved, so let's just say that too: we are often wrong, and always loved.

If you ask me to confess something
I'll answer like a job interview:
Oh, I'm a perfectionist. I try too hard.
Who, me? I spend too much time
compensating for the faults of others.
It's exhausting.

Yes, I do try too hard, too long,
weary myself.
And this loving heart has
been broken by others
too many times to count.

But I might also add:
I want the world to cost me nothing.
I nurse grudges and nurture
my own entitlement.
I want things I shouldn't have
and desire praise I haven't earned.

I would do ugly things if I could
look good doing them.

I do not give as easily as you ask me to
and pour out my gifts with an open heart.
I don't.

And when I do, I make sure
everyone knows it.
I have done things I should regret
but loudly tell people they were
"learning experiences."

Lord, help me hold these hard truths
up to the light.
Help me admit them without falling
into a tar pit of shame.
Remind me that the light of your truth
is searing,
burning up every bit of ugliness.

Teach me that when I confess
you are healing me, changing me,
showing me the burden of a lie
and the power of the truth.

So here I am, God. Shine your light.

---

reflection prompt

*Perhaps this might be our simple
acknowledgment for the day: we are often
wrong, and always loved. Always, always loved.*

for making all things beautiful

I sought the Lord, and he answered me; he delivered me from all my fears. Those who look to him are radiant; their faces are never covered with shame.

—PSALM 34:4-5 (NIV)

I spent about two years getting some form of chemotherapy or immunotherapy on a weekly basis, and it showed. I looked pale and puffed up with fluids. I lost feeling in my feet, so I would often stumble, and when I fell, the small cut would bleed for days. I didn't feel tired, exactly; I felt *weary.* Like someone who might lie down and feel so entirely weighed down by life that I might never feel ready to get up.

But there is something I started doing that I have never grown tired of trying. Because I felt entirely cut off from the land of the living, if I walked by a store I found myself staring at the window displays papered with glossy advertisements. I was confronted by a kind of beauty I could never again possess, and I would feel a terrible mixture of awe and fear. *They* were beautiful. And I was *this.* I tortured myself this way until I decided one day to try something new. I stopped looking at the storefronts entirely (I forbid it!), and I would search the faces of the people walking by. They were laughing or tired, pushing a stroller or talking on the phone. And I knew at all once that they were beautiful. *We* are beautiful. All this effort, all this living . . . we are radiant somehow.

I am only skin and tired bones.
I am familiar aches and endless
to-do lists.

Thank God, then, that
when I am weak, you call me strong.
When I am unclean, you call me pure again.
When I am tarnished, you call me shining.

You are making all things beautiful.
You are tapping on all the windows
and the doors
so that I will fling them open.
Let your light in, God,
and cast the darkness out.

I will stop looking in the mirror
and start seeing you in your people.
I will pause from these unfinished labors
and see you at work instead.
I will hear your song singing
through all the things you've made,
the people you've hung on my heart
like an anchor.

Here we are, God, your people.
Beautiful.

reflection prompt

Search the faces of strangers and friends.
Photos on the mantel. At the grocery store.
Aren't we beautiful?

overwhelmed, stressed, overwhelmed, stressed

**Teach me the way
I should walk.**

—PSALM 143:8B (BSB,
ABBREVIATED)

This is where it all breaks down: time. Our hours and minutes and days. Too often we are propelled through life at a speed that prevents us from pouring everything we need into these tiny increments of time (Tuesdays in particular). Researcher Brené Brown suggests that, at this point, it might be helpful to ask yourself if you are stressed or overwhelmed. If you're stressed, you will feel the burden of so much pressure but continue to muscle through. You might take some small actions to remedy it. But if you're overwhelmed, you have reached a level of stress that renders you incapable of anything for the moment. As Brown observes, "When we say we're overwhelmed, it's really telling our body, 'Things are happening too fast. We can't handle them. Shut down. Shut down.'"

Have you been feeling stressed or overwhelmed lately? God, bless us here in that feeling of being overwhelmed and wanting to love others regardless.

No matter how much planning,
anticipating, making lists,
there are always daily fires.
When is the appointment?
There's been a delay at the pharmacy,
the pickup line, the checkout counter.
Who needs to pick up groceries again?
Pack, bathe, rummage, drive, launder, call.

Somewhere at the center of me
is this love that whirs.
It ticks like an atomic clock.
I will love them all hours and my days.
Every calendar page can be told as a story,
thousands of dates and times,
that I love them, show up for them,
care for them.

But, Lord, somewhere at the center of me
is an alarm bell, ringing.
This rare and precious life you give,
all my hours and my days,
are being carefully placed into boxes
and packed away by this schedule,
these errands,
these acts of good, good service.

No matter how much forethought,
working ahead, "life hacking,"
I will never finish it all.
So give me a fresh sense of urgency.
When is the sunrise?
Read me a poem.
Who here has an amazingly
embarrassing story?

There will need to be a delay
at the pharmacy, the pickup line,
and the checkout counter.
You are giving me back this day.

reflection prompt

One of my favorite comedians, Tina Fey, once described this state perfectly as feeling "blorft." "Blorft is an adjective I just made up that means 'completely overwhelmed but proceeding as if everything is fine and reacting to the stress with the torpor of a possum.'" What do we learn about God and ourselves when we feel blorft that we wouldn't have learned otherwise?

Third Sunday of Lent!

No, seriously. Take a nap.

letting yourself be known

I hide myself in you.

—PSALM 143:9B (NIV)

In an era of social media disclosure, everyone is rushing to be known. What kind of coffee do you like? You already posted about it. What did you think about the last election? You gave everyone a few insights to chew on. Having trouble with your kids? We can tell. Or if you worry that no one cares, just check in with your friendly neighborhood multibillion-dollar tech company. You are *known*. They care! Somewhere out there is a customized algorithm with your height, weight, location, shopping preferences, and which roads you take to work. Terrifying. Eerie. Disorienting.

But who really knows us? Sometimes I can hardly tell. Most of my faults I try to hide. And most of my genuine attempts at connection are limited. So perhaps we might think about what we keep to ourselves. What do we hide? Can we imagine a God whose ability to see and know us inspires a sense of relief?

I work quietly, in secret, to repair
all that is broken.
This anxiety and *that* despair.
(Other problems I avoid altogether.)

There is no use telling you, I reason.
This is mine to fix.

But your eyes see everything, God.
Why can't I see that as the gift it is?
But I am seeing you, fixed from above
with the pixelated precision
of drone warfare.
Your omniscience would be terrifying,
exhausting to imagine,
or, worse, humiliating.

But you come from below, Jesus.
Bleary eyes in a manger.
A steady gaze as you walk among us.
Or stare straight from the cross.

You look at me with nothing more,
nothing less, than with the love that first
interrupted my life with your existence.

There is no protecting you from me.
Or me from you.
From my insecurities and apathy,
from the shrug of my shoulders
when you say that you are here
to love me in aliveness.

Nothing is hidden from you, God.
You can see it all.

What a gift, God.
What a gift.

reflection prompt

*We can have a very Elf on the Shelf view of God
at times.* THERE IS GOD WATCHING YOU.
*Shudder. What image of God seeing you and
caring about you could you find comforting?*

letting go is painful

I give them eternal life, and they shall never perish; no one will snatch them out of my hand.

—JOHN 10:28 (NIV)

Who are you? Are you the person you were last year? The one who had *that thing* happen? Are you somebody's daughter or somebody's mom? These are such layered kinds of questions because they attempt to offer a single, brief answer to a seemingly endless thought. Who am I? Well, probably 256 roles at the moment. But when we are attempting to let go of something painful, it is a question we return to again and again. Who am I now?

The poet Maggie Smith has a lovely image for this impossible question that I find useful. She wonders if perhaps we can think of ourselves as a series of nesting dolls, those wooden matryoshka dolls where each figure is hiding another identical, smaller one. Smaller and smaller they go down to the tiniest, the size of a thumbnail. "Think of yourself as a nesting doll: how many versions of yourself have you carried this far, to this point? How many more iterations will there be as you age? Know there is room for all of you." When you need to let go of some pain, perhaps it is a good time to bless all the versions of you. You are not eclipsed. You are not lost. You are here.

I have tried to keep, preserve—
place between tissue paper,
seal into frames—
everything precious.
I have tried to repair, replace
everything broken.
I am cataloging memories
with an archivist's eye.
Nothing will chip or stain
or be misplaced somewhere,
at someone's house, and be
forgotten altogether.
Nothing will slip away.

Lord, I couldn't bear to lose any more
than what's already gone.

But then, God, the children wiggle out of
favorite clothes
with each passing year,
and there are boxes of Grandma's things
in the attic.

He left, and she's gone,
and my closets are stuffed to the ceiling
with reminders:
we are losing the life we knew;
we are gaining a life we didn't imagine.

We are picking up and putting down.

So let's take the china out of the cupboard,
the baseball gloves out of the garage,
or whatever tells our story.
And tell it.

We will not be lost.
We will never be lost.

reflection prompt

*Let's bless all of those selves, all the way down
to the tiniest one. Can you name some and give
them a good BLESS YOU?*

regret

**As far as the east
is from the west,
so far has he removed
our transgressions
from us.**

—PSALM 103:12 (NIV)

Do you believe in regret? That is my friend Sascha's favorite question at parties and oooooo weeeeee does she get some hot sauce answers. "Absolutely!" "Absolutely not!" "Yes, but don't ask me why." "Are you telling me I should feel bad?" The question conjures up immediate vulnerability. It asks people to make a decision about the aftermath of a mistake. Confession? Embarrassment? Self-administered amnesia?

Most people stick to the party line: "I couldn't possibly regret what I've done . . . because it made me who I am today." But that's not a very convincing argument. Yes, there is no question that our mistakes shape our lives. But we might say something more redemptive instead. "I regret what I've done . . . and what I learned since has made me who I am today." Now, the person who said *that* is someone I want to take to dinner and pepper with questions. Who are we becoming even though we always have something to regret?

I would go back, God,
to the moment it happened.
No. To the moment before that.
I would rewind this pain like a cassette.
The person who made that decision—
who was that?
They never existed at all.

But, instead, here we are. Downriver.
Carried by the currents of circumstances
and my own damn choices.
Lord, I want to undo what's been done
and unwrite this story.
Take me back, take me back,
make me someone else entirely.

Grief. Embarrassment. Shame.

Since we can't go back, Lord,
pull me forward. Remind me of the
surreal truth that you unwrite any sin.
I confess and you forgive.

Your love is simple. Clean.
You really do take me back
to that moment of decision
or circumstance
and can make me someone else entirely.
My worst moments are written
in disappearing ink.

Love. Relief. Mercy.

Now pull me to my feet, God.
If I need to apologize, help.
If I can't apologize, help.
If I am not forgiven, help.
Thank you for helping me become
someone else, someone new.

reflection prompt

What's your first answer to Sascha's party question? Too much regret, and we are mired in shame. Too little regret, and we are stuck in denial. This is the oddest prayer prompt I have ever written, but I think it's the right one: Can we pray for the right amount *of regret?*

not knowing the next step

Ask for the ancient paths, ask where the good way is, and walk in it, and you will find rest for your souls.

—JEREMIAH 6:16B (NIV)

It is always hard to see the purpose in wilderness wanderings until after they are over.

—JOHN BUNYAN, *THE PILGRIM'S PROGRESS*

I have come to truly despise the quote by J.R.R. Tolkien that reads: "Not all those who wander are lost." It's taken from a beautiful poem in his Lord of the Rings trilogy, and it is certainly true, but by the time I read it on a sign hanging on someone's trailer wall it had lost most of its magic. You are on vacation, people! You are supposed to wander! I am trying to get somewhere and failing, which makes me both *wandering and lost*.

Perhaps that is why John Bunyan's allegorical book *The Pilgrim's Progress* is one of the most widely read works in the English language. It follows a man who knows he must take a journey with God and is endlessly waylaid. Our confusion, our distractions, our burdens are constantly threatening to cause us to despair and turn back. What is next, God? And why can't I get where I need to go? Let's bless our need for both comfort and another step, knowing that so often we are both wandering and lost.

God, here's the thing.
I've done all that I know to do.
I've thought of every possible solution
and it's still not okay.
So let me be blunt:
will it always be this way?

Will I wander around in the unknowing,
where every solution proves temporary
and every problem becomes another?
How will I know if I am making progress
or where to go next?

I need to know what the greatest good is,
and how to live into it.

Maybe, God, it is simply this:
if I desire and love the good
that I know how to do
(however incomplete it is),
the next step will be toward you.

You will meet us where we fall short.
When we fall headlong down
the wrong rabbit holes.
When we need strength for our burdens
and healing for our brokenness.

I may not know the answers,
or the best possible next step,
but I do know the sound of your voice.
I am wandering, Lord, without destination,
except that I know you are always with me.

---

reflection prompt

*What is the next right step that seems obvious
to you? Or even a tiny bit obvious? Write it
down or put it in your calendar. Take courage.
You're on your way.*

for trusting your own intuition

But the wisdom that comes from heaven is first of all pure; then peace-loving, considerate, submissive, full of mercy and good fruit, impartial and sincere.

—JAMES 3:17 (NIV)

How do we trust our own intuition? For many of us, that is a difficult task. Our intuition can be crowded out by self-doubt. It can be shouted down by the voices of others—or those whose opinions we have internalized. We can begin confidently down a path only to find ourselves spun around by our own insecurities. Perhaps we also have the sense that our best ideas are compromised somehow. Too many self-interested desires are clouding what was supposed to be pure.

In such times, we might borrow inspiration from the mystics and monastics, those who know how to expertly quiet distraction and attend to the voice within. First and foremost, they cultivate a practice of shutting their faces. Closing their pie holes. Zipping it. That's right, they get very quiet. It's horrible (she said, as a natural talker). But perhaps we can bless the desire to calm our hearts and see if we can trust what's already inside of us.

So, God, it's strange that sometimes
in the middle of an ordinary conversation
the volume dial of my intuition
begins to rise.
It starts with a faint hum, a vibration,
and the twinges of awareness
that there's something else I should be
paying attention to.
Something beyond
the transactional nature
of what is being said.

I keep listening, within and without,
and more and more
my interior voice grows louder,
signaling frantically like a coach
on the sidelines,
then beginning to shout.
And I remember.
Pay attention. Grow still inside.
Listen.
Is that you? Are you teaching
me something?

Is that my own fear or self-loathing?
What is wisdom and what is simply
the echo chamber of my own mind?

Bless me as I learn how
to shift my awareness,
to grow in wisdom and in peace.
Root me in kindness toward
my own unsettled heart
and thank you for teaching me
that somewhere,
in my own heart and mind
and body and soul,
good truths are being told.

You live in me.
What a wonder.

---

reflection prompt

Writer Margaret Silf gave this advice for those who want to try: "In the silence of our hearts, we must wait patiently for the compass needle to steady. Then it will point to true north, the still center . . . and we will be enabled to move forward again." Imagine that needle within you shaking and then starting to still. Breathe. Listen.

to see clearly

**Lead me in the way
everlasting.**

—PSALM 139:24B (NIV)

The best prayer I can imagine is simple: God, help me see things as they really are. Help me know what is evil so I can participate in what is just. Help me see what is good so I can jump in and facilitate good. Help me know my own heart (which is a little bit terrible, and a whole grab bag of wonderful). If I can see things clearly, I can be many things. But I won't be deluded.

It turns out that there is a wonderful word for that: *prudence.* Prudence is the wisdom to discern. So often mistaken for mere caution, it is a virtue of distillation. When we have seen the truth and we learn to draw careful distinctions, then we are becoming skilled at the seemingly boring art of prudence. So this is a blessing to help us see the world as it is so we might be able to say: Ahhhh, I see it now.

Yes, we will grieve,
but not as those in denial.
We will suffer,
but not as those entombed in loneliness.

We will join the ranks of the afflicted,
the weak, and the vulnerable.

We do it willingly. (Okay, not always.)
But you are showing us what is plastic
and what is gold.

Blessed are we, looking to you, God,
and to Jesus, our friend,
in the dawning of that unshakable kingdom
we know but cannot see.
Lead us there.

We would choose self-preservation
at all costs

if you had not given us a glimpse,
a preview that reminds us that evil always
destroys itself in the end.

Now that we've seen it,
we have learned the true value
of what needs to be hated—
disarmed without cruelty or disdain—
and what needs to be cherished.

We will carry forward only what is true
and good and beautiful,
knowing this: love never, ever fails.

reflection prompt

*In what situations do you feel like you always
have clarity? What do you suspect helps you
keep that perspective?*

Fourth Sunday of Lent

Rest. Please take a break.

feeling anxious and criticized

So if the Son sets you free, you will be free indeed.

—JOHN 8:36 (NIV)

I wish that the phrase "don't take criticism personally" was actually a cure for taking criticism personally. All the best advice suggests that criticism is an opportunity to pause, listen, and respond. All the worst advice suggests that we should internalize, flail around, and take every bit of criticism as an indictment of our true intentions. Great. But honestly, I need a little love and compassion before I can begin to know what is true and what is not. If you, like me, need a moment of love before our better angels take over, this blessing is for you.

Oh, the power of a word, letters, syllables,
squeezing me into a small, terrible space
with someone's singular judgment.

Someone has summed me up,
tied me in a bundle,
and moved on.

And in that temporary confinement
I strain a little, and call out,
"Wait a minute!"
But my voice doesn't sound quite right.
I struggle to make a move,
but for some reason the criticism
still holds.

I am trapped, Lord,
here in the words that aren't
teaching me anything
but embarrassment and anger
and more than a little self-hatred.

Every criticism feels like a knife
with a blade at both ends.
Every time I try to yank it out,
I open a fresh wound.

God, your verdict on my life is love.
If there is something terrible,
awful I need to change,
you will nudge me, prompt me,
not in the voice of my worst critic.
You tell me as a friend.
You tell me what is and has ever been true.
It is gentle and complete,
yet breaks every chain.

Quiet my self-critical heart,
leave what reminders are there
for my good,
and free me from all that makes me forget
the joy and freedom of having you
as my only judge.

reflection prompt

*Who makes (or made) you feel deeply
understood? Forget your critics for a moment
and imagine that they are here with you. What
loveliness and limitations do they see in you?*

feeling meh

**Behold, God is my helper;
The Lord is the sustainer
of my soul.**

—PSALM 54:4 (NASB)

How are you? Perhaps the answer is a shrug. We can find
ourselves in a wonderfully neutral place ("I'm fine! Stop asking!"),
or perhaps it is a sign of having shut down.

So how are we really? Apathetic. Tired. Overwhelmed. Not sure
how to ask for help. There is a good chance that when we come to
the end of our words, we need a little (or a lot of) divine assistance.
If you are feeling beyond your limits, or are numb at the thought of
trying, let's bless that sense of stuckness.

After striving, after exhaustion,
or maybe after I barely tried at all,
I feel nothing, God.
Nothing terribly inspiring.

I always imagined that, at the very least,
I would be the person who *tries*.
Or at least *tries to try*.
But there's not a lot
to work with here, God.
Not joy or repentance.
Not hope or sorrow.
Honestly, if someone didn't remind me
that apparently I am deeply committed
to loving you,
I might have forgotten.

So what can you do with that?

Perhaps you might begin with the fact that
I paused now at all.
Or the fact that feeling nothing
is a welcome break
for a heart like mine.
Or perhaps you'll place a little sticky note
on the mirrored surface of my mind
which reads:
"100% Guaranteed Human."
You know. You knew.
If, in moments like this, I grow first tired,
then numb,
you will wake me, rest assured,
with the gentlest hello.

reflection prompt

Numbing is the body's disconnect from the possibility that something might overwhelm. Maybe pain. Maybe too much of a good thing. It's not fun, but it is a clue that we need downtime that might lead to rest. Go for it.

for a very busy day

The Lord himself goes before you and will be with you; he will never leave you nor forsake you.

—DEUTERONOMY 31:8A (NIV)

Do you remember the comic strip *Calvin and Hobbes*? This boy and his stuffed tiger had an upside-down cardboard box that was, on closer inspection, a Transmogrifier machine capable of transforming or multiplying any object into something else entirely. Don't want to go to school? No problem. Calvin transmogrifies himself into an army of Calvins capable of doing every unwanted task. I keep wondering if God's real mistake in creation was in not making us capable of replicating and dividing ourselves. Someone *else* could go to work. And I could finally go to Paris! DREAMS ABOUND! NAPS ARE PLAUSIBLE!

These little fantasies are part of our natural protest against our limitations. We don't want to be stuck in our busyness. We want more and we can't seem to create it inside hours that don't multiply. So perhaps we can take a second and forgive ourselves for not transmogrifying. And bless whatever is possible instead.

I'm climbing, step by step, to the top of this
very full and busy day.
Each step is a thought, a plan,
a preparation, a catch in the breath.

And like a kid at the top of
the playground slide,
I just sit down and stop,
because I know that in a moment
I'll have to lean forward
and assent to the momentum that is latent
in all these plans.

Here at the pivot point,
alternatives suggest themselves:
wouldn't you rather . . .
isn't this a little . . .
what were you thinking?

And then I remember that time has
a habit of surprising me,
the way it stretches or shrinks
or turns itself inside out,

revealing treasures
I couldn't have imagined
or barriers that invite a total rethink.

So the only thing to do is
to ask you to bless the flow
once I let go.

Bless it with presence of mind
to talk to you in real time,
ask you questions,
and listen underneath
for the reality that you are here,
and most interested in who I become
in the meantime.

---

reflection prompt

Okay, but for real: If you could have another
version of yourself, what would that self be
doing? Sometimes our little fantasies help
shake loose a dream. My other self would live in
Paris, and she is a diplomat. So, wait, maybe I
should try to relearn French. What dreams are
bouncing around in your head?

feeling God's love

**I have loved you with an
everlasting love;
I have drawn you with
unfailing kindness.**

—JEREMIAH 31:3 (NIV)

Think back. Was there a time and place where you have felt truly *beloved*? I mean, downright cherished? Those are precious and good moments. Sometimes it's the feeling of your dog or cat deciding you have hung the moon, or at least put dinner out in a dish. A child who hugs you around the waist. A friend's irrational interest in the specifics of your day. (Is any Thursday really that interesting? Probably not, but I'm not complaining.) It could be an anniversary celebration, a graduation moment, or the feeling of someone squeezing your hand. We forget these moments quickly, but they are crucial. If we forget what it feels like to be loved, we may not remember how to be loved by God too.

Let's try.

God, it has taken a while to see it,
clouded as these days have been
with a vague sense of unease,
gradually coming to my awareness
that I need to feel your love.
Not generally. Not for the whole world.
But for the specific, particular me
that is here, now.
(Though it feels embarrassing to say so.)
But aren't we all at the center
of our own stories?
As heroes, villains, winners, losers,
or whatever fits the plot of the day?

God, rewind this story
back to the beginning,
when my eyes opened and, newborn,
I came into this world wholly loved.
You loved me.
Not for anything I had done,
but simply *because*.

And here, though my vision is blurry,
I do know what love feels like.
And that is life to me.

So remind me again, God,
how the world spins and the winds change
and the oceans churn and not a single fact
tells a different story
than your love for me.

reflection prompt

*I have a spectacular friend named Chelsea, and
we have known each other since we were in an
elementary school judo class. We are true
witnesses to each other's lives, so we are
forever talking about what goes on "The List."
The List is our shorthand for saying: What
experiences really* count*? When something
lovely happened, did it go on The List? So
here's a bit of spiritual homework, friend. Let
the next good thing that happens to you* really
count*. Let it be part of the story of how loved
you really are.*

for the pain that lingers

He will wipe away every tear from their eyes, and death shall be no more, neither shall there be mourning, nor crying, nor pain anymore, for the former things have passed away.

—REVELATION 21:4 (ESV)

George Orwell once observed that "of pain you could wish only one thing: that it should stop. Nothing in the world was so bad as physical pain. In the face of pain there are no heroes." We may despise our weakness, but then we find ourselves twisting in our beds, on hands and knees in the bathroom, or wincing when we think no one can see us. And then there is the mental pain, psychological fissures that break into our consciousness. We find it impossible to get up, take a shower, put away *those* thoughts, stave off a looming fragility. And we think, *Make it stop. Please, God, make it stop.*

My dears, these are the truths we cannot say at parties . . . that, so often, we are laid low. We are humbled, humiliated even, by having lost all control for a moment. We feel scared that it won't end, and confused about the future. This is the hard road of pain. So this blessing is for us.

Blessed are you,
trying to live with the pain that lingers.

A body that won't heal,
won't stop hurting,
won't shut up.

An emotional wound that won't close,
won't stop aching
and you wince at every touch.

A person who won't accept solutions,
won't offer back words of kindness,
who persists in willful misunderstanding.

Lord, I thought that being a "good person"
would solve the problem of pain.
But here I am.

Will you stitch together what feels like
brokenness into something whole?

Blessed are we, living with what is,
living into courage we didn't want to learn.

Blessed are we, finding a radical acceptance
of the intolerable, the absurd,
the unwanted.

We are forgoing ease for wisdom,
accepting the deepest kind
of self-knowledge
that we can be healed while in pain,
whole while broken,
loved while rejected.

It's here. It's true. I can see it.
You have made me a kind of miracle.

reflection prompt

*We do not always know how to endure the pain
that lingers. But we know that it includes some
kind of radical acceptance of our finitude, even
as we know we fight on. So let's pray for a bit of
that acceptance, shall we? God, help me
accept my fragility. And promise you will hold
me together.*

feeling too much, be back later

Pour out your hearts to him.

—PSALM 62:8 (NIV)

Do you consider yourself a sensitive person? There are a few traits to consider: Do we easily feel the hurt of others? Do we experience emotions with intensity and find ourselves deeply stirred by the news or other people's problems? Well then. That sounds like a sensitive person to me. But it's not exactly a socially acceptable fact to declare to others. We might have heard people respond with a "Don't be so sensitive!" Rarely do the nonsensitive types get a scolding for caring too little. They just look, well, *cool*.

Sensitivity, however, is a two-sided coin. It connects us to all that is around us, or could be. It makes us aware and awake to the beauty and tragedy of the human experience, but that awareness comes at a steep cost. So if you are feeling the two-sidedness of this gift right now (and probably mostly the cost, if we're being honest), then this blessing is for you.

I know it. You know it.
We are one of the sensitive ones
who live amid the constant low hum
of overconnectedness.

Like a computer program running secretly
in the background,
it takes up memory, space.
It buzzes with a light tingly feeling
that feels a little like fear, or vigilance,
functioning like a sign in a shop window:
"Open for Business."
Lord, I feel too open
to people, ideas, plans, and dreams,
and all the things that aren't happening
but could be.
Always available. Always too aware.

So how about it?
How about just for a day we turn
the sign around
to show what's on the back:
"Closed!"
And feel that sigh that comes
when it rings true

that the one thing necessary for now
is to lock the door.
Not accept the pain of the world
as our own.
Not feel every joy and sorrow
like a full-time job.
But click off the lights and say,
at least to ourselves,
Be back later.

---

reflection prompt

*Pretend you have one of those old-school
pagers (the precursors of cellphones that
people used to clip onto their belts). Someone
can ping you at any time, but you can't ping
them. Imagine all the people who could buzz
you, and everything they want. Whew.
Overwhelming. Now think of a few by name
and send them a quick mental Bless you. Now,
look. You need a little mental break. So shut off
your mental pager for a certain number of
hours. Perhaps turn your actual cellphone on
silent if you dare. Good job. Now stay "offline"
for a set amount of time so you can recharge
your lovely self.*

for Palm Sunday

A very large crowd spread their cloaks on the road, while others cut branches from the trees and spread them on the road. The crowds that went ahead of him and those that followed shouted,

"Hosanna to the Son of David!"

"Blessed is he who comes in the name of the Lord!"

"Hosanna in the highest heaven!"

When Jesus entered Jerusalem, the whole city was stirred and asked, "Who is this?"

The crowds answered, "This is Jesus, the prophet from Nazareth in Galilee."

—MATTHEW 21:8-11 (NIV)

Jesus, from that mountain
high among the olive trees,
it would have been an easy walk
down to the city,
to Jerusalem, which lay below.
So why choose to make your way
on a donkey,
on an everyday beast of burden,
your feet almost dragging on the ground?
And who are these people running,
bending low,
to spread their precious cloaks
on the road before you,
waving palm branches and shouting,
"Save us! Hosanna to the Son of David!"?
What is the raw and urgent hope that rises
in their songs?
"Blessed is he who comes
in the name of the Lord!"
And, Jesus, why are you smiling?

Because it is true what they are saying,
though they can't yet know the whole of it.
It is happening. It is unfolding
in slow motion,
the fulfillment of that promise from of old:
their savior would come,
humble, and riding on a donkey.

Blessed are we, on this side of history
shouting, "Come, Lord, save us too!"
We know how it ends, and *still* we forget
to rush toward our humble,
forgettable king
and yell, "Hosanna, hosanna,
our hope is in you!"

reflection prompt

There's something incredibly embarrassing about yelling adoration. Have you ever done it? But it's honest in a way that is difficult. We risk something in our hope. Think of a time you saw God popping up in any part of your life, big or small, and try a little "Hosanna." Superquietly is fine. When we double down on genuine gratitude, we become a little braver. (And a little more awkward. Three cheers for the awkward!)

compassion, suffering alongside

When Jesus saw Mary's profound grief and the moaning and weeping of her companions, He was deeply moved by their pain.

—JOHN 11:33 (VOICE)

Blessed are you, the sensitive one,
attuned to the feelings of others.
You couldn't turn it off if you tried.

Blessed are you with
the emotional bandwidth
to hear hard things,
without fixing or minimizing or deflecting.
You know the gift of presence.

Blessed are you who choose to show up
without judgment,
with little gifts
or small acts of practical help.
You know the gift of compassion.

Blessed are you, too, when you are
utterly exhausted by
other people's problems.
(And actually, now that we're
talking about it,
it's getting even more annoying.)
Your empathy is a precious gift
that deserves to be protected too.

Today, help me stand
ready to hear those divine whispers
nudging me to give compassion away.
Naturally. Freely.
And help me find those who,
to my surprise,
want to pour back into me
(which, *fine,* you know I hate receiving).

Love given and received,
without shame or embarrassment.
Because what *else* can a bighearted
person do
but learn to give and get?

reflection prompt

The week before Easter we think a lot about Jesus's deep humanity. His soon-to-be-scarred hands. His loneliness. His compassion. In what way does your humanity make you more *(not less) like Jesus?*

you need help in real time

Hear, O Lord, and answer me, for I am poor and needy. Guard my life, for I am devoted to you. You are my God; save your servant who trusts in you.

—PSALM 86:1-2 (NIV, PARAPHRASED)

It's me again, God.
You know the difficulty I'm in,
and how helpless I feel in this web
of circumstances.

You, above all, can see all
the hidden factors,
and what is possible in this moment.

I need help in real time,
now in this present suffering,
and step by step as events unfold.

Come and be with me right here
in this small space where I am stuck.
Show me what agency I do have.

God, blessed am I with a mind
to behold you,
revealed in Jesus,
ever living, ever one with you,
with the world ever weighing on his heart.

I feel entirely helpless
and unable to dictate terms.
So . . . whatever. (Can I say that, God?)
I just need help right now.
I need your compassion and love
to be active in practical ways,
to move into what has been unmovable
for so long,
to be the change I need,
that the world needs.

Clear a path. Make a way. I need you now.

reflection prompt

*During these days leading up to Jesus's death,
we feel his dread, his fear, his helplessness. And
we feel our own. Do you have a "help!" prayer
you want to try right now? It's the simplest
kind and usually the last one I reach for.* God,
seriously, help me.

good news is hard to find

Many are asking, "Who will show us any good?"

—PSALM 4:6A (NLV)

Oh, God, this world and its peoples
are hurting,
and everywhere we look
there is something to lament.

And here at home,
there are fresh disasters
where recovery will be slow,
and some things are just gone now,
never to be restored.

We look for hope
that peace could break out,
that the hungry could be fed,
and those in pain relieved
of their suffering.
That parents would not fear
for their children
nor leaders, their citizens.
And on and on.

God, when will relief come?
When will death be swallowed up forever,
and all tears be wiped away?

When will come that promised time
of everlasting joy,
and all things be made new?

Let me sense you with me, here in this
unfinishable life.
I must heap these burdens
(my arms are full of them)
into your willing hands.
Show me how I can be like you
in the improbable and creative
and even irreverent ways
that you staved off
the ugliness around you.
How you surprised us all
with the reality of life.
God, somehow, let this day be a sign
of good things to come.

---

reflection prompt

*Where do you look for a sign of good things to
come? Nature? Family? Friends? Cat videos? If
nothing comes to mind, take a walk or scroll
through your photos. Let yourself think,* AHA!
*when you see the first lovely bit of hope. We
will need every bit of light to see in the dark.*

when we say no to God

Jesus was troubled in spirit and testified, "Very truly I tell you, one of you is going to betray me."

His disciples stared at one another, at a loss to know which of them he meant. One of them, the disciple whom Jesus loved, was reclining next to him. Simon Peter motioned to this disciple and said, "Ask him which one he means."

Leaning back against Jesus, he asked him, "Lord, who is it?"

—JOHN 13:21-25 (NIV)

Jesus, we watch in awe, in horror.
You sit down with your friends to dinner
to eat with those who give you up.
They will seek payment for your death.
They will deny knowing your gentle voice.
They will turn away when the hardest part
comes.

Knowing this, you bend to them.
Wash them. Serve them. Feed them.
Saying, "Take, eat, this is my body,
broken for you."
Saying, "Take, drink, this is my blood,
shed for you."
To be given for them? For us?

God, this is a new thing,
this kind of self-giving
that offers what we need
before we know we need it,
before we are able to understand
or receive.

And then it happens. You give in.
Deceit and greed and lies win the day.
You are silent as those you love
hand you over
to willful violence, eager to hide from you,
the light, shining on them
so inconveniently.

We don't know it, Jesus,
but you will feed us, wash us,
serve us, save us.
And we will do our best to set you aside.
But this is your great stubbornness:
how you give us what we need, even as we
refuse it.

---

reflection prompt

Many of us, when faced with something good,
instinctively step back. No, thank you. Stop
looking at me, complimenting me, loving me,
helping me. This is a day in the Christian year
when we are getting ready to admit that we
will say no, even to God. Let's pray: God, you
never step back from us, even in our refusal.
Help us learn to be better at being loved.

for Good Friday

He said to the Jews, "Behold your King!" They cried out, "Away with him, away with him, crucify him!" Pilate said to them, "Shall I crucify your King?" The chief priests answered, "We have no king but Caesar." So he delivered him over to them to be crucified.

So they took Jesus, and he went out, bearing his own cross, to the place called The Place of a Skull, which in Aramaic is called Golgotha. There they crucified him, and with him two others, one on either side, and Jesus between them."

—JOHN 19:14B-18 (ESV)

To the cross, that's where love led you.
So that's where we come too,
to stand and grieve with Mary and John,
your mother and your closest friend,
overwhelmed that it should come to this:
powerlessness and utter loss.

So much hope and healing
and laughter and feasting
and miracles and promises
have come to this.
To untold suffering, and a cruel death.
It is finished.
In the darkness, a figure comes
moving cautiously,
hands reaching up to ease your body down.
And women with their spices and linens,
gently doing for you what they could,
helpless with grief as they lay you
in a tomb.

What's this? The strongest have come,
Roman soldiers enacting orders
to seal off the entrance permanently.

Blessed are we who remain here in wonder,
in the stillness, with the silence of death
so heavy upon us,
asking again, "Jesus,
is this how it goes?
Is this how love wins?"

reflection prompt

Jesus's violent death stands in front of us as an impossibility. How can the savior die? And, really, how can the ugliness of death visit each of us? The feeling is one of horror. Allow yourself to think about the horror of it for a moment without turning away. This is what we do during Holy Week: we do not flinch from the truth.

for Holy Saturday

As evening approached, there came a rich man from Arimathea, named Joseph, who had himself become a disciple of Jesus. Going to Pilate, he asked for Jesus' body, and Pilate ordered that it be given to him. Joseph took the body, wrapped it in a clean linen cloth, and placed it in his own new tomb that he had cut out of the rock. He rolled a big stone in front of the entrance to the tomb and went away.

—MATTHEW 27:57–60 (NIV)

Nothing happened. Have I got that right?
Nothing happened at the cross.
We're still here, in the mess and confusion.
It's all over and we're all left to ourselves.
Can such be the narrative when we
remember your words:
"In a little while and you will see me no
more. Again a little while and you will
see me."
Okay. But in the meantime,
where are you, Lord?
It is so quiet for us here,
we who are still overwhelmed by the
darkness of what evil accomplishes.
And for so many, life just goes on.
But for us, who sit in the valley
of the shadow of death,
we cry out: "Where are you?"

But then we remember something.
Maybe it was in prophetic words of old,
or maybe it was something in your look
or in your touch
when you healed or forgave or
stood there for hours teaching
or gathering up
the small and weak and sick in your arms.

And somehow we know, that darkness
is but light to you
and that even now you are
still on the move—
moving on down, down to the depths
of every hell,
to free us to spend eternity with you.

Jesus, you came down from heaven,
yes, but then you kept coming down,
down to the sick and the poor,
the lost and forsaken,
down to the utterly brokenhearted,
because that's who you are.
That's what you do.
So we wait.

---

reflection prompt

*If you have ever been left waiting without an
answer to prayer. If you have been holding the
heaviest burden or intractable pain and
wondered,* So what now? I'm supposed to
just . . . wait here? Suffer here? Forever? *Today
is the great acknowledgment of all those of us
who wait. If this were a movie of the cosmic
drama, we would see the screen split. We
would see the buried savior, awaiting
resurrection; the believer standing utterly
alone, believing God is dead.*

Easter Sunday

Now Mary stood outside the tomb crying. As she wept, she bent over to look into the tomb and saw two angels in white, seated where Jesus' body had been, one at the head and the other at the foot.

They asked her, "Woman, why are you crying?"

"They have taken my Lord away," she said, "and I don't know where they have put him." At this, she turned around and saw Jesus standing there, but she did not realize that it was Jesus.

He asked her, "Woman, why are you crying? Who is it you are looking for?"

Thinking he was the gardener, she said, "Sir, if you have carried him away, tell me where you have put him, and I will get him."

Jesus said to her, "Mary."

She turned toward him.

—JOHN 20:11–16A (NIV)

So, Jesus, wasn't that illegal
for you to break the seal
the Roman guards put there?
Bursting the bonds of death itself
to come again, larger than life?
And was it wise to present yourself
first to the women,
so lowly in social standing their word
meant nothing in court?
And why did you keep appearing suddenly
to the huddled believers
behind locked doors for
fear of their enemies,
scared out of their wits to hear you say,
"Peace be with you!"?

And isn't it the case that they were
never the same again,
these ordinary people
who had been so cowed,
receiving your Holy Spirit,
emboldened to begin the work you
set in motion,
speaking life and health and peace
to all who would listen?

This is what our newborn church
looks like: Blessed.
Blessed in our fear and inadequacy.
Blessed by your faith in us.
Blessed that we received,
by your own hand, the gift of hope—
the beginning of the end of sin
and of death.
We follow you as best we can
along that downward path
with all the humility we can manage.
You came back to us.
Alleluia.
Alleluia.
Alleluia.

reflection prompt

*The downward path. Does it hurt? Can it
embarrass you? Is it absurdly inconvenient?
Yes, yes, and yes. But also we are learning to
tell the story of our lives. We are loved. We are
strengthened even when we feel undone. We
learn to serve even as we ask for help. What
has the downward path looked like for you?*

LENT IS OVER, LOVELIES!

Have a Beautiful, Terrible Advent!

What Is Advent?

Advent is that beautiful stretch of time leading up to Christmas. The season is approximately four weeks before Christmas (the actual number of days varies every year), and the feeling, always, is anticipation. Unlike Lent, which mixes anticipation with dread and hope, Advent is like watching a slow dawn. God will appear on earth but not as we expect. The ruler of the universe will come, not as a philosopher-king or a warrior-sage, but as a helpless child. We thought we might be awed by a savior's majesty, but instead, this Jesus melts our hearts. We feel his smallness, his helplessness, and the disarming sweetness of our love for him.

Advent is a season of charity and conscience and hospitality. We are all welcome precisely because our savior wasn't. We tell the story of an immigrant family, no room in the inn, rulers who want him dead. For this reason, the history of Christmas has been full of rituals and practices of social inversion, upside-downness. My historian dad, Gerry Bowler, has written all kinds of wonderful books about Christmas, so I've been hearing about these Christmas customs all my life. Rich and poor, young and old, insider and outsider switch places. Then for a moment we see something we have forgotten for the remaining eleven months of the year. And then we remember the words of the gospel of Matthew: "The last will be first." Yes. We are learning to see God's kingdom come.

This gentle heartbeat that animates Christmas is also why Advent is not simply beautiful. It causes our hearts to ache. This season of love reminds us of when our children were little, when our grandparents or parents were alive. We set the table for an extra setting without thinking, *Oh, they are gone.*

If this Advent is sweet or bittersweet, this season is for you. I am including a longer scripture passage drawn from the lectionary, which tells a part of the story, and a brief reflection question. There is an entry here for each of the four Sundays of Advent—hope, love, joy, peace—and for the bigger moments too. There are blessings for Christmas Eve, Jesus's birth, Christmas Day, and Epiphany. Technically, the "Advent season" ends on Christmas Eve, and then we have a whole separate "Christmas season" (twelve days of Christmas!). But I've mushed them together for your convenience.

Don't tell my dad.

for hope

And do this, understanding the present time: The hour has already come for you to wake up from your slumber, because our salvation is nearer now than when we first believed.

—ROMANS 13:11 (NIV)

There is a story you are telling, Lord,
about the way that time itself
bends toward you.
How a baby being born shone a light
that set wise men on their course
and kings wringing their hands
and calling for blood.

You are changing the world.

But first we must understand that
our hope is a force
set in motion at the dawn of time itself.
It was you who began that long descent
from the heights of heaven
as creator, as love, as a promise
come down to us at Christmas.

You are an improbable blaze of glory
that was one tiny infant,
to become one of us
in all human sense and feeling,
and become for us our sure
and certain hope
that one day, all sadness and sorrow
will flee away,
and death will be no more.

Come, Jesus.
We are ready to learn hope.
We want to be told, once again, that
before light was separated from darkness
and mud shaped into life
you've been waiting to say: "I am here."

reflection prompt

Hope *is one of the most powerful words we
have. It has so many synonyms (faith, trust,
belief), but none are quite right. How do you
define hope? And where do you see it?*

for love

Show me your ways, Lord, teach me your paths. Guide me in your truth and teach me, for you are God my Savior, and my hope is in you all day long. Remember, Lord, your great mercy and love, for they are from of old. Do not remember the sins of my youth and my rebellious ways; according to your love remember me, for you, Lord, are good.

—PSALM 25:4–7 (NIV)

It is the first truth we learn.

We sing it as our song.

We are love.

We are love.

We are made for it.

When it's absent, we feel brittle.

When it's withheld, we feel starved.

It is food and wine and Halloween candy.

God, we feast on it.

So when you say,

"Behold, this is my son,"

it feels right, pre-known,

that he would come as love itself.

Jesus, I already knew you.

You are the first truth I already knew.

You are love.

You are love.

We are made for you.

---

reflection prompt

Imagine you are telling a friend about how this Advent season has been. Where did you feel love? Where did you feel its absence?

for joy

And Mary said:
"My soul glorifies the Lord
and my spirit rejoices in God my Savior,
for he has been mindful
of the humble state of his servant.
From now on all generations will call me blessed,
for the Mighty One has done great things for me—
holy is his name.
His mercy extends to those who fear him,
from generation to generation.
He has performed mighty deeds with his arm;
he has scattered those who are proud in their inmost thoughts.
He has brought down rulers from their thrones
but has lifted up the humble.
He has filled the hungry with good things
but has sent the rich away empty.
He has helped his servant Israel,
remembering to be merciful
to Abraham and his descendants forever,
just as he promised our ancestors."

—LUKE 1:46–55 (NIV)

God, we are feeling
the spark of anticipation,
the delight, that gives us the tiniest inkling.
We are beginning to understand the truth:
joy is our natural habitat, our real home.
And just maybe, somehow,
you are making a way for us to live there
already.

Jesus, we're craning our necks to see more.
But that's as far as we can stretch for it.
You are going to have to bring a little
heaven down closer to us.

And show us more of this reality we sense
but can't yet quite comprehend:
that hope fulfilled will become
our foundation,
love our shelter, and joy the air we breathe.

Blessed are we who say,
"Come, Lord Jesus, and come soon.
You are filling our hearts to overflowing."

reflection prompt

Where is the pull toward joy in your life now?

for peace

Restore us, O God;
make your face shine on us,
that we may be saved.

—PSALM 80:3 (NIV)

God, we long for peace,
but we have already drawn our blades.
We are at war with each other,
and within ourselves.
Our world—the evidence of our folly—
on full display.
We waste away in quarries
dug by our own hands.

Oh, Jesus, come to us.
Come suddenly, into the center
of our deepest need.
Come swiftly into the chaos of
our conflict and distress.
Establish the peaceful order of your rule,
not ours.

Your kingdom, not ours.
Reign with sovereignty in our hearts,
which refuse correction.
Reign with power over
all that is ungovernable.
Reign with mercy over our communities,
our neighborhoods, and our nation.

Blessed are we who look to you, Jesus,
to be the change we cannot enact.
Come, prince of peace,
to our bleeding world.

reflection prompt

We long to be more than thoughts-and-prayers people. We want to be thoughts and prayers and action peacemakers. What kind of peacemaking can you be a part of in this season of your life?

for Christmas Eve

While they were there, the time came for her to deliver her child. And she gave birth to her firstborn son and wrapped him in bands of cloth, and laid him in a manger, because there was no place for them in the inn.

—LUKE 2:6–7 (NRSVA)

You are here. What a wonder.
Robed in the everyday majesty
of a newborn,
so beautiful, so soft, so new.
Perfect in the terrifying fragility
that thrills every parent.
("Watch his head!" "Look at those
tiny fingernails.")
God become human,
blinking at strange, new surroundings.
All wisdom and power
poured into a smallness
that knows hunger and gravity
and unseen urgency for your mother's skin.
And Mary, so newly parted from you,
turns her thoughts to the impossible
angelic visitation that promised
you'd come.

And she knew, somehow,
staring at your eyelashes,
that you were a great reversal,
here to put all things right.

Blessed are we when our hearts
warm with her.
You're here. And we are too,
newly come to worship
with kings and shepherds
and barn animals and angels
as you light up the world on
this holiest, loveliest night.

---

reflection prompt

Advent calendar chocolates. Presents under the tree. Cards in the mail. What has brought Jesus's birth into your home this year?

87

Jesus's birth

In the beginning was the Word, and the Word was with God, and the Word was God. He was with God in the beginning. Through him all things were made; without him nothing was made that has been made. In him was life, and that life was the light of all mankind. The light shines in the darkness, and the darkness has not overcome it.

—JOHN 1:1–5 (NIV)

This is the beginning for us,
but not for you.
You were there with God
from the beginning.
No, wait, from before that.
From the vastness of eternity
without beginnings or ends.

As Creator of all that is,
Redeemer in eternal intention,
and now in historical fact.

It is you who are launching this
new start for us,
this new reality that you come to reveal,
for it is by your light
that we see the world as it really is,
and the truth of it all,

That though the mighty of this world
may grasp power for a time,
their thrones are shaky and will fall.

That though the wise of this world
may hold sway for a season,
their words will be washed away
like sandcastles on the shore.

Blessed are we who rejoice to know that
the powerful of this world are as nothing in
the presence of true majesty.
You are love eternal,
present to us yesterday, today,
and right to the end.

Blessed are we who say,
Lord, yours is the light that draws a line
between every good and every harm.
You have come and now we can only
shake our heads in wonder
that today, on the birthday of your life,
your story is our own.

reflection prompt

Emmanuel *means "God with us." This is the
name that the prophet Isaiah used to describe
the savior to come. When do you feel that
around Christmas? For me, it's the moment
someone lights a candle and sings* "Silent Night."
Geez Louise. It's my favorite. What's yours?

for Christmas

And there were shepherds living out in the fields nearby, keeping watch over their flocks at night. An angel of the Lord appeared to them, and the glory of the Lord shone around them, and they were terrified. But the angel said to them, "Do not be afraid. I bring you good news that will cause great joy for all the people. Today in the town of David a Savior has been born to you; he is the Messiah, the Lord."

—LUKE 2:8–11 (NIV)

We are Christmas people.

Light in the darkness, Christmas people.
Ruler of the universe born as a baby.
Inversion of the world on a starry night
kind of folks.

We are Christmas people.
Expectation amidst sorrow.
A strong suspicion that empire,
in the face of true divinity,
will cry, CRUCIFY HIM! CRUCIFY HIM!
But first we must talk about shepherds
and wise men.
We will bow down before him.
After all, we saw the star.

Our story is of a refugee family
and no room in the inn
and the murder of the innocents,
so we string up lights

and declare that Jesus
steals into every darkness.
He does.
He does it so we can see.

Christmas is the faint light of
transcendence
—not the blinding beams of the impending:
HE WILL COME AGAIN AND NOW HE IS
RISING INTO HEAVEN.
On Christmas, he's a baby,
our ember.
Glowing.
Glowing.
Glowing.

reflection prompt
The shock of the baby and not the king-on-a-throne has forever marked our faith. How is God unexpected in your life?

for wisdom

When they had heard the king, they set out; and there, ahead of them, went the star that they had seen at its rising, until it stopped over the place where the child was. When they saw that the star had stopped, they were overwhelmed with joy. On entering the house, they saw the child with Mary his mother; and they knelt down and paid him homage. Then, opening their treasure-chests, they offered him gifts of gold, frankincense, and myrrh. And having been warned in a dream not to return to Herod, they left for their own country by another road.

—MATTHEW 2:9-12 (NRSVA)

Wise men.
They followed a star to where you lay,
tiny king.
Wonderfully ordinary
in the sounds you made,
perfect in the way all babies are,
but worshipped by important men,
wise men bearing gifts,
looking, searching, plotting trajectories
and making plans that,
once they were sure the signs were right,
they'd follow.

Blessed are we who are searching,
looking for the signs,
desiring above all the star, the wisdom,
the light by which we might see.
In our time, in our world.

God, can the light of that star reach us,
these thousands of years later?
And how would we know it,
the fact of your coming?

It seems hard to see in the broad daylight,
but, oh, how it meets us in the dark
from light-years away.
All creation knew it:
the star at your birth,
the seas at the sound of your voice,
the darkening skies at your death,
the gladdened hearts at your sweet return.

God, blessed are we who bow in the dark,
feeling our way forward in the unknowns
to wait and watch for the pinpoint of light
that will be your gift to us.

---

reflection prompt

*We may go through very dark seasons when it
seems impossible that any light could reach us.
We stumble, we bleed. I love the image of that
ancient star whose light reaches even us.
Where can the light find you today?*

acknowledgments

One of the strangest parts of survival is the cost. *How much? Whoa, for how long?* The enduringness of hardship never ceases to surprise me. And also, sorry, exactly how does productivity work when everything unravels?

People. It turns out that people are the ticket to making it through, so I have many of them to thank for helping me pay all that creativity (and pain) demands.

Toban and Zach. Your gorgeous faces stuffing cereal into your gobs in the morning light. Nothing is more precious to me than you. And my extended family, oh boy. It turns out that it's possible to be *too* grateful because I can't stop weeping while saying grace at our family dinners. Katherine, Bart, Ellie, and Evelyn Smith, my life with you is complete.

Thank you to Gerry and Karen Bowler, my intrepid parents, for all the work they poured into the foundation of this book. I am so proud to be your daughter.

Jessica Richie. You deserve a full-page glossy photograph here under the heading "Best Friend Makes Tragic Year Productive!" You boss, produce, cheer, email, write, and partner like no one I have ever met or will again. My favorite joke is when I say "I love you" and you hang up.

I have a truly magical team at *Everything Happens* who loves ministry for some reason, and I couldn't do it without them. Harriet Putman, Brenda Fitzgerald, Hope Anderson: you launch a book like no one in human history. Thank you to Jeb Burt, Keith Weston, Dan

Wells, Chris Howell, and Kristen Balzer. A very special bit of gratitude goes to Gwen Heginbotham for her graphic design and visible repulsion at bad serifs.

I have an incredible work life filled with good-hearted and high-fiving partners and friends. Thank you so much to my agent, Christy Fletcher, and to the team at Convergent for your relentless enthusiasm: Tina Constable, Campbell Wharton, Keren Baltzer, Karen Fink, Alisse Goldsmith-Wissman, Rachel Tockstein, and Cindy Murray. The Everything Happens Center at Duke University has been enthusiastically championed by Clay Robbins, Dennis Campbell, Robb Webb, Chris Coble, Verity Jones, Edgardo Colón-Emeric, Dave Odom, Jim Heynen, Angela Graham, Vince Price, and Kavin Rowe. Thank you, thank you.

Thank you to *Comment* magazine for allowing a version of the essay "The Roof Always Caves In" in their October 2022 issue to appear in these pages.

Chronic pain is an absolute beast, and these people encouraged me with tireless (but surprisingly not annoying) optimism: Sascha Seinfeld, Sarah McHale, Heath Carter, Gary Haugen, Sam Wells, Sarah Bessey, Jeff Chu, Katherine and Jay Wolf, Moe Rivera, Anne Snyder, David Brooks, Andrea Westbrook, and Jon Scheyer. (Note: Caring about Duke basketball is very time consuming so I probably shouldn't thank Jon from a productivity standpoint, but dang is he encouraging.) Joel McHale, no one gives a better pep talk than you. Not a soul. Consider joining Cameo? Chelsea Jalloh, the world's only perfect person, you walk this earth and so nothing can be all that bad. And Dr. Haider Warraich, you gave me permission to keep living in the midst of so much unending pain. We borrow courage from others, don't we? I know of no other way.

scripture credits

about the author

Kate Bowler is the three-time *New York Times* bestselling author of *Everything Happens for a Reason (And Other Lies I've Loved)*, *No Cure for Being Human*, *Good Enough*, *The Lives We Actually Have*, *Blessed*, and *The Preacher's Wife*, and hosts the popular podcast *Everything Happens*. A Duke University professor, Kate earned a master's of religion from Yale Divinity School, and a PhD at Duke University. She lives in Durham, North Carolina, with her husband and son but consistently brings up the fact that she is Canadian and spends the summers there.

about the type

This book was set in Macklin Text, a contemporary serif created by French type designer Malou Verlomme in 2020. Macklin Text was inspired by early nineteenth-century European typefaces, especially the work of British typefounder Vincent Figgins.

More from
KATE BOWLER

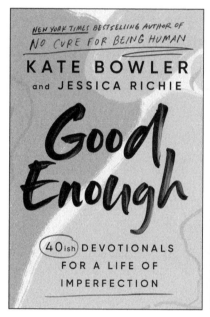

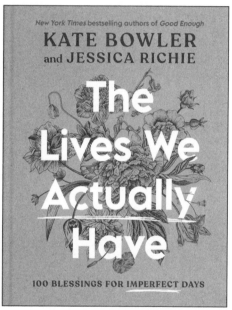

CONVERGENT

Available wherever books are sold

- I am healthy, I am strong, I am safe
- together we grow, together we flourish

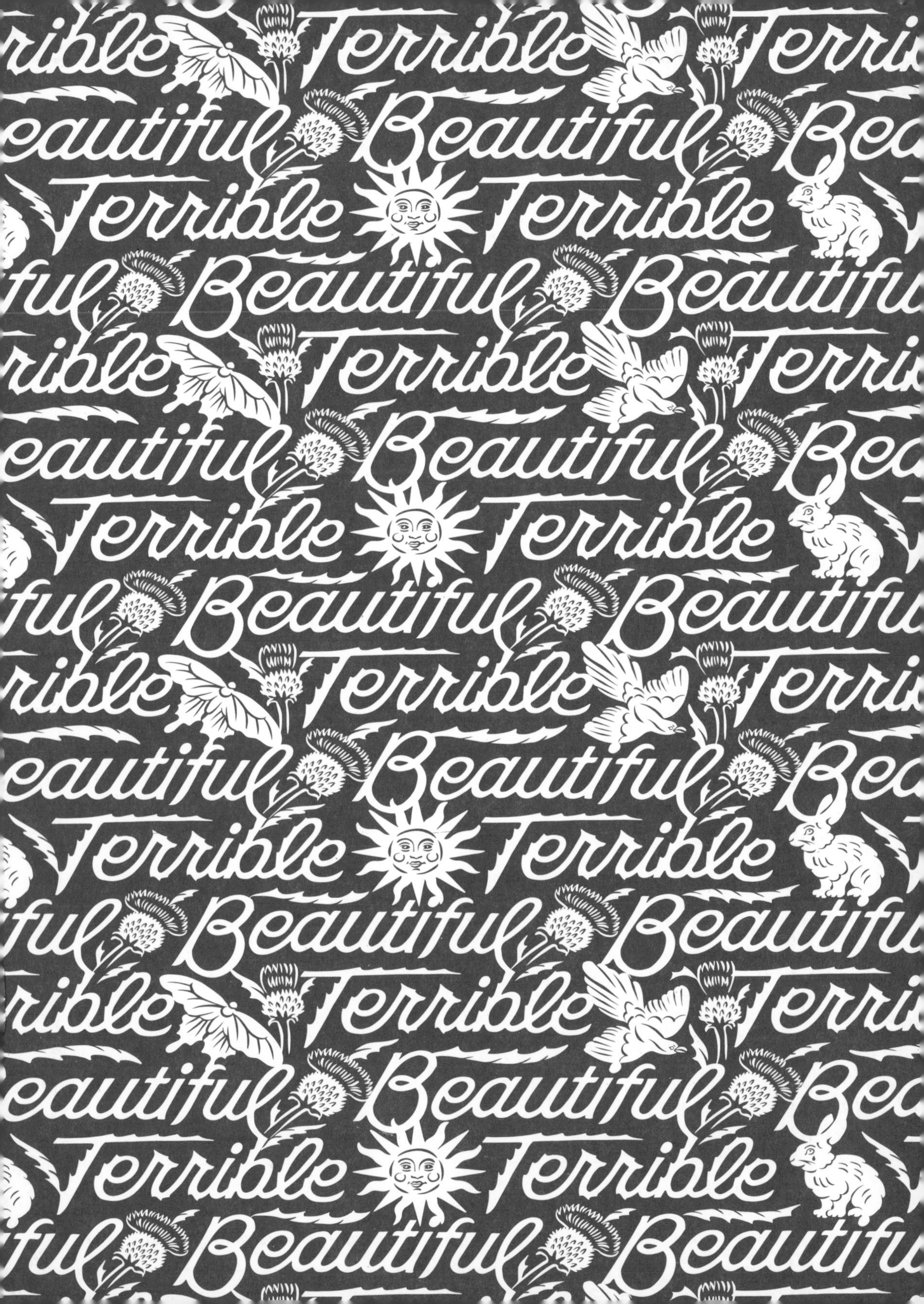
Terrible
Beautiful